New Approaches to Rural Policy

LESSONS FROM AROUND THE WORLD

ORGANISATION FOR ECONOMIC CO-OPERATION AND DEVELOPMENT

ORGANISATION FOR ECONOMIC CO-OPERATION AND DEVELOPMENT

The OECD is a unique forum where the governments of 30 democracies work together to address the economic, social and environmental challenges of globalisation. The OECD is also at the forefront of efforts to understand and to help governments respond to new developments and concerns, such as corporate governance, the information economy and the challenges of an ageing population. The Organisation provides a setting where governments can compare policy experiences, seek answers to common problems, identify good practice and work to co-ordinate domestic and international policies.

The OECD member countries are: Australia, Austria, Belgium, Canada, the Czech Republic, Denmark, Finland, France, Germany, Greece, Hungary, Iceland, Ireland, Italy, Japan, Korea, Luxembourg, Mexico, the Netherlands, New Zealand, Norway, Poland, Portugal, the Slovak Republic, Spain, Sweden, Switzerland, Turkey, the United Kingdom and the United States. The Commission of the European Communities takes part in the work of the OECD.

OECD Publishing disseminates widely the results of the Organisation's statistics gathering and research on economic, social and environmental issues, as well as the conventions, guidelines and standards agreed by its members.

> *This work is published on the responsibility of the Secretary-General of the OECD. The opinions expressed and arguments employed herein do not necessarily reflect the official views of the Organisation or of the governments of its member countries.*

© OECD 2005

No reproduction, copy, transmission or translation of this publication may be made without written permission. Applications should be sent to OECD Publishing: rights@oecd.org or by fax (33 1) 45 24 13 91. Permission to photocopy a portion of this work should be addressed to the Centre français d'exploitation du droit de copie, 20, rue des Grands-Augustins, 75006 Paris, France (contact@cfcopies.com).

FOREWORD

Odile Sallard, OECD
Thomas Hoenig, Federal Reserve Bank of Kansas City
Margaret Clark, The Countryside Agency
Charles Fluharty, Rural Policy Research Institute

More than 120 senior policy officials and experts from 15 countries (including all G7 countries) gathered at the Airlie Center near Washington, D.C. on March 25 and 26, 2004 to discuss the future of rural policy. This international conference was convened by the Federal Reserve Bank of Kansas City, the Organization for Economic Co-operation and Development (OECD), the Rural Policy Research Institute, and The Countryside Agency. A welcoming address was made by Constance A. Morella, Ambassador of the Permanent Delegation of the United States to the OECD. Keynote speakers included Alan Greenspan (Chairman, Board of Governors of the Federal Reserve System, United States) and Donald J. Johnston (Secretary-General, OECD). Other speakers included Nicolas Jacquet (President, Delegation for Economic Development and Regional Planning, France), Oryssia J. Lennie (Deputy Minister of Western Economic Diversification, Canada), Gianfranco Miccichè (Deputy-Minister of the Economy, Italy), David Sampson (Assistant Secretary, US Department of Commerce) and Antonio Sanchez de Rivera (Deputy Minister for Social Development, Mexico).

OECD countries have felt the sweeping changes that globalization is bringing to the industries that have long fuelled rural regions. Developments in technology and transportation have resulted in improved market accessibility and substantial increases in efficiency. At the same time globalization has yielded widespread consolidation in commodity industries, with significant effects on competition and pricing. Today, external competition, changing patterns of consumption and other economic and social drivers mean that rural areas can no longer depend solely on traditional forms of industry and employment for their livelihoods.

We acknowledge that agriculture will continue to play an important role in our economies and shaping our landscapes, but agree that agricultural policy can no longer be the primary instrument of rural policy. Support for agriculture does not automatically equate to support for rural people and businesses. Subsidies are expensive, particularly when they tie a region into a particular activity or discourage investment in other sectors. To address the depopulation and economic loss in rural areas we must look for new opportunities to spur prosperity.

During this conference our discussions focused on a crucial question now facing developed nations throughout the world: How can public policy help rural regions build new sources of economic growth in rapidly changing global markets? We are starting to reach agreement on the increasing need for countries, regions and localities to diversify their economic activities to compete in the global and national economies. Experience from around the world has shown that regions can do this successfully, but many rural areas in virtually every country face great challenges in doing so.

The role of policy makers is to design policy that accommodates the varying circumstances across rural areas, avoiding a one size fits all approach for development. Experience has shown us that one common element among rural areas that thrive is their ability to utilize and promote endogenous attributes and comparative advantages. The challenge for policy makers and delivery bodies is to develop less prescriptive approaches, allowing rural communities and businesses the flexibility to identify and respond to their local needs.

The development of innovative rural policy relies heavily upon the nature of its design and implementation. This will require changes in governance and the development of new relationships across the public, private, NGO and philanthropic sectors, with actors that have very diverse values, power bases, skills, resources and responsibilities. The next generation of champions for these new approaches will have to be open to integration as it will be a driving and sustaining force in this shift.

While there are still many questions that remain unanswered, the many successful experiences and innovative approaches discussed during this conference are very encouraging. Further steps will need to be taken toward improving the future of rural policy and this will require our continued work together. On behalf of our organizations we look forward to sharing this information with the hope that it will provide some important 'fuel' for the global debate on rural policy and will contribute to its advancement.

TABLE OF CONTENTS

FOREWORD 3
ACKNOWLEDGEMENTS 7
PREFACE 9
CONFERENCE CONCLUSIONS 11
PART I: THE NEED FOR NEW RURAL POLICY 13

    The New Economic Imperative in Rural Regions
        by Donald Johnston 15
    Thinking Regionally in a Globalizing Economy
        by Alan Greenspan 21
    Prosperity and Productivity
        by David Sampson 27

PART II: THE RURAL POLICY LABORATORY 31

    New Regional Partnerships in the United States
        by Gilbert G. Gonzalez 33
    Rural Entrepreneurship: A Cooperative Case Study
        by Bob Militello 39
    The Micro-Region Strategy in Mexico
        by Antonio Sánchez Díaz de Rivera 45
    Linking Rural Policy and Regional Development in Western Canada
        by Oryssia Lennie 49
    Reducing the Territorial Divide in France: Redefining Regions
        by Nicolas Jacquet 55
    Federal Co-ordination in Austria
        by Wolf Huber 61
    The Living Countryside in the Netherlands
        by Kees de Ruiter 67
    Rural development in Europe: Approaches and Future Perspectives
        by Francesco Mantino 69

PART III: THE FUTURE OF RURAL POLICY 89

    Five Themes in the Future of Rural Policy
        by Mark Drabenstott 91

Where is Rural Policy Headed?
  by Sergio Soto Priante 95
Challenges for the Future of Rural Policy
  by Richard Wakeford 97

ANNEX A: CONFERENCE PROGRAM 101

Tables

Table 1.   Intervention measures 72
Table 2.   National vs. regional competences in rural development 79

Figures

Figure 1.   Distribution of rural development resources 73
Figure 2.   Rural structural v. environmental modernisation 75
Figure 3.   Modernisation measures in relation to holdings' structure 75
Figure 4.   Distribution of R&D resources 77
Figure 5.   National vs. regional distribution of RDP resources 80
Figure 6.   The dispersion model 81
Figure 7.   The unbalanced model 82
Figure 8.   The balanced model 83

ACKNOWLEDGEMENTS

This conference was organized by the Organization for Economic Co-operation and Development, the Federal Reserve Bank of Kansas City, the Rural Policy Research Institute and the Countryside Agency.

Special thanks are given to Mark Drabenstott, Vice-President and Director of the Center for the Study of Rural America, Federal Reserve Bank of Kansas City, Nancy Novack, Associate Economist at the Center for the Study of Rural America, Federal Reserve Bank of Kansas City and Marcie McLaughlin, Director of National Policy Programs at the Rural Policy Research Institute for their work in organizing the event.

The conference organization and proceedings were directed by Mario Pezzini, Head of the OECD Territorial Reviews and Governance Division, and co-ordinated by Nicola Crosta, Administrator and Linda Adamson, Consultant both of the OECD Territorial Reviews and Governance Division.

PREFACE

Ambassador Constance Morella
Permanent Delegation of the United States to the OECD

It is impressive that participants from more than 15 countries gathered here to discuss the future of rural areas. This meeting brought together senior policy makers as well as representatives from the business and academic sectors. All are linked by the common objective of improving the effectiveness of rural development policy and a shared conviction that a new policy approach is needed to respond to the challenges and opportunities of globalization by releasing the potential within rural areas.

I am pleased to note that the United States is not alone in its commitment to find solutions to the challenges facing rural areas. We know that rural regions are not doomed to depopulation and economic decline. Rural areas possess significant resources that are often misused or under-utilized. The presence of natural and cultural amenities, high value local products, and the availability of land are only some of the intrinsic assets of rural spaces. Such richness corresponds to an increasing demand from urban populations for safe, high quality food; open, well-kept landscapes and spaces; and a protected environment in which to live, spend free time, or set up business. On this premise, growth in rural areas can be built while benefiting the nations' population as a whole. However, to achieve these goals we cannot rely on agriculture alone as a source of new jobs or as an anchor to attract young people to stay, instead we need to re-think rural development policies.

The issue is truly of global interest and the level of participants at this conference demonstrated the strong commitment from policy makers across OECD countries to devise better policies to foster competitiveness and avoid depopulation and job loss in rural areas. Another resource is the OECD's work on territorial development which provides a valuable platform for comparing and analysing regional economic development policy from a multi-sectoral perspective.

This conference provided an opportunity to take advantage of the diverse expertise found amongst the participants, and to attain an even better appreciation of the challenges that rural areas face. We have recognized that change is inevitable and now it is time to transform ideas into action. In this way we can help create a new, more prosperous future for rural regions everywhere.

CONFERENCE CONCLUSIONS

Globalization, the emergence of important new niche markets, and freer trade bring both threats and opportunities to rural regions. Many rural regions suffer from lagging economic growth and still depend heavily on commodity industries, such as agriculture. Globalizing markets diminish profits in these industries and encourage businesses to consolidate.

Participants agreed that new policy approaches are needed to help rural regions compete effectively in rapidly changing global markets. This will demand a shift away from past reliance on subsidies focused on a single sector, namely agriculture, towards an integrated place-based policy for rural development. This shift will allow rural regions to contribute to overall economic growth by seizing new opportunities.

While globalization brings special challenges to rural regions, it also unlocks bright opportunities. Recent innovations around the world demonstrate that rural regions are not doomed to depopulation and economic decline. Rural areas often possess valuable resources that are largely underused. Natural and cultural assets, high value local products, both agricultural and non-agricultural, and the availability of land are only some of the endowments of rural spaces. Information and communication technologies provide rural areas with tremendous new opportunities in economic development and public service delivery.

Faced with these challenges and opportunities, conference participants agreed that developed countries need to forge new policy approaches to spur economic development, innovation and productivity growth in rural areas. Many countries lack a comprehensive rural development focus. Policies remain largely concentrated on supporting low-cost agricultural commodities and are often characterized by a redistributive logic. In the future, rural policy should shift to an integrated approach focused on the distinct demands and assets of rural places, and to public actions that spur private investment in those places. Conference participants stressed the importance of investing in 1) human capital, by increasing the skills of rural inhabitants; 2) infrastructure, by insuring the connectivity of the rural areas in the new economy; 3) social capital, by facilitating partnering and knowledge pooling across and within levels of government—and between the public and private sectors. It was agreed that these are the main preconditions for strategies to extract the value of cultural and natural resources and to foster business clusters that tap niche markets for products and services.

Several countries have begun to design new policies and to promote innovative forms of governance to implement them. These experiences mark a breakthrough past the traditional top-down, sectoral approach to rural development. They demonstrate the adoption of a holistic approach that integrates scattered policy initiatives into a comprehensive framework, showing a shift towards "new rural governance" based on consultation, negotiation, and partnerships among government, businesses and communities. They are shifting away from a past reliance on subsidies and towards promoting new investments in countryside renewal. The common theme in many of these policy innovations is their emphasis on exploiting underused assets, releasing potential, fostering entrepreneurship and mobilizing private investment. There is also an increasing awareness in governments of the need to use a 'rural lens' to safeguard the interests of rural residents and businesses.

Charting a new course for rural policy will provide guidance for the rural regions throughout the world that are not seizing the opportunities offered by new technologies and free trade. It will require new relationships with urban residents and policy. By better harnessing distinct rural assets and spurring investment, the new policy approaches will boost rural economic growth and reduce the need for government subsidies to compensate for development gaps. Recognizing the challenges posed by new approaches to rural development policy, conference participants agreed on the need for continued exchange of lessons learned and welcomed the offer made by the Mexican Government to host an international conference on rural development in 2005.

PART I: THE NEED FOR NEW RURAL POLICY

The New Economic Imperative in Rural Regions
by Donald Johnston

Secretary General
Organisation for Economic Co-operation and Development (OECD)

The issues of rural development and the decline of the farming population are very much at the top of all of our agendas. Productivity in the private sector has increased dramatically everywhere, in some countries more than others. By and large the percentage of people working on farms today is much, much reduced.

Productivity was a central focus at a forum in China in 2004, with participants discussing different initiatives to increase productivity. Currently there are 800 million Chinese working on farms and Premier Wen anticipates that between 500 and 600 million of those individuals will be leaving the farms within ten years. While substantial population movement into urban areas will be an issue, the more immediate concern will be to provide sufficient opportunities within the rural communities in China.

This is not just an OECD issue. However, it is very important for the OECD, as a community of advanced and industrialized nations, to improve our own economies as well as to serve as a very good example for other countries such as China and other nations that find themselves in this very challenging situation.

After years of decline, a new vision of the future of rural areas is taking shape. This new vision is based on diversified rural economies that combine a fresh look at rural industries with better development of the economic potential of natural and cultural assets. This must also be coupled with the pursuit of new activities that can make rural areas competitive in the global economy. In this respect, the Information and Communication Technology (ICT) revolution provides rural areas with a tremendous opportunity, perhaps an even greater impact than we initially anticipated.

I would like to delve into a few aspects of rural policy. First, the profile of rural areas is dramatically changing. Contrary to widely held assumptions, "rural" is not synonymous with agriculture or at least not any more. Agriculture now represents less than 9% of employment in rural regions of OECD countries, and it is the major employer in only 3% of these regions. However "rural" is neither synonymous with decline. Over the period 1990-2000, on average, rural regions lagged behind urban areas in growth of both per capita income and employment. But some rural areas performed very well, even better than urban areas, namely the mountainous province of Aosta in the Alps which has the highest per capita income in Italy.

Second, I would like to discuss ways to leverage rural assets through innovative policies, particularly addressing new rural policies and the strategic role of networking and partnerships. It is important to underline that in many cases, the economic success of rural regions has been based on capturing global markets. The rural area of Ibi near Valencia in Spain doubled its employment base when it became the national capital for the production of toys. Castellon de la Plana, in the same region, is now the world leader in the production of ceramic tiles. In the United States two hundred firms in the carpet industry support the economy of the small city of Dalton, Georgia. And hosiery firms clustered in the Piedmont region of North Carolina produce a large portion of the socks and stockings sold in the United States. Rural areas across the OECD are benefiting from these types of niche market concentrations.

The questions that policy makers in OECD countries want to answer are why do certain rural regions perform better than others? What is the key? What have been the most successful strategies to attract investment and create jobs? And what innovative ways are there to leverage rural assets?

Clusters

As one might guess from the aforementioned examples, specialisation in clusters is often the key. Over the past four decades, an unexpected economic miracle has taken place in some rural areas. Relatively backward rural economies have been transformed into prosperous industrial poles. These cases, cited in the United States and Europe, are but a few of the small towns and regions where small firms, belonging to the same economic activity or sector, have settled into a concentrated area. When I was Minister of Economic Regional Development in Canada, we all wondered why the region of Beauce, Quebec, was so successful, only later recognizing that it had benefited from an unintentional cluster.

Examples of this trend can be found in many member countries. The Bank of Italy recently demonstrated that firms located in clusters in Italy have rates of return on investment and on equity that are, respectively, two and four percent higher than those of firms outside such cluster areas. Being in clusters gives firms a number of advantages that can be turned into productivity gains: a larger market for workers with specialised skills, more rapid information flows and knowledge diffusion, and relations of trust between contracting agencies, which encourages specialisation. The US has also noted a strong potential for strengthening rural clusters across the nation. The synergy within clusters is reminiscent of Robert Hutton's theory on the value of social capital, a product of the facilitation of commercial relations outside formal labour frameworks.

Local amenities

Key assets in rural areas are a clean environment, attractive landscapes, cultural and, particularly in Europe, gastronomic heritage. Potential economic opportunities include green tourism packages and promoting local products. By cultivating their natural and cultural assets regions have the opportunity to improve their per capita income.

Increasing demand for high quality natural products, and growing awareness of the environmental risks of certain types of agriculture, provide opportunities for rural regions to "capture" the value of their amenities. Farmers can participate by producing quality agricultural products or developing niche markets such as bio-farming which can generate significant additional resources. In England, the rural population is growing in absolute as well as in relative terms because people are moving back to the countryside to take direct advantage of these amenities. Amenity-based development also gives farmers opportunities to diversify their farm-related activities, by playing the role of "Guardian of the environment".

ICT

An OECD report published in 2001 on ICTs and rural development concluded that, with targeted training of the workforce, new job opportunities in fields such as call centres, data processing, product design and software development can be created. Scotland is often cited as an example of how such industries can successfully locate in regions that were previously considered to be too remote or peripheral.

These ICT-based industries do not need to be large scale in order to make an important difference in local life, and public policy can provide useful support. For example, we reviewed the case of a small declining farm town in North Dakota that created a "Technology Center", as a multi-purpose facility to house businesses, offer day care for young working parents and supply ICT training. This Centre reversed the previously negative image of the town and stimulated the return of entrepreneurs that had left the area.

Rural development cannot take place without some prerequisite conditions such as connectivity, availability of public services and permanently upgraded skills. The overall attractiveness of an area for working and living rests on the availability and quality of public services. Public service delivery in rural areas is a critical "chicken and egg" issue. Often a dwindling population justifies the closure or reduction of facilities such as schools, health care centres and even post offices, but this in turn triggers more departures or discourages new inhabitants from coming to the area.

Maintaining minimum levels of accessible public services in low-density regions is a daunting challenge which requires innovative solutions. Efficient transport infrastructure is obviously important, but I would like to underline the enormous potential of the use of information technology. For example telemedicine, in my home country of Canada, as well as in a number of countries, has proved to be an efficient and economical solution to meet the needs of settlements situated far from major urban centres. Populations of the Indian First Nations, in particular, now receive quality health care through specialist consultations via the Internet.

The delivery of high quality education in rural areas is of great importance. In order to respond to new possibilities, rural residents need to be equipped with new skills. As rural economies evolve, so do the skills requirements of local industries. The internet will undoubtedly make an important contribution to education provision. But in some countries, notably in the US and Canada, local higher education institutions, frequently known as community colleges, are also playing a major role by acting as a link between local industries, particularly SMEs, and the local labour force. In addition to their role in developing skills, many are important centres of innovation and technology transfer acting as isolated local business systems. These community colleges are proving to be an invaluable development resource for many rural regions.

New rural policies and governance

Traditional rural policies were mostly geared towards agriculture, with a strong emphasis on direct subsidies delivered top-down. It is important to note the distortions that these policies have created is due to the fact that they are poorly integrated with the objectives of other sectors such as small business development and basic infrastructure implementation.

Now the new rural policy emerging in all OECD Member countries deals with rural development as a whole: the agricultural component fitting into a more synergistic, wider picture. There is an emphasis on cross-sector co-ordination and the definition of real customized local strategies. Agriculture must be a component within these strategies, but it must not be addressed outside of other issues.

As the use of subsidies declines, there is an increasing need for regions to identify their competitive advantages. Some regions are leaders in different manufacturing activities. Others base their development on attracting new activities, or marketing local products and services, or attracting new residents with an exceptional natural environment. Other communities can look to advantages in terms of rapid links to major urban areas. Some are investing in regional education institutions.

These plans require a new approach to policy and a major re-think of the governance arrangements for policy delivery. The OECD governments are taking a number of innovative steps to improve administrative structures. First, local actors from the private as well as the public sector are becoming more involved in project definition and implementation. Across the OECD we see innovative institutional arrangements to build partnerships that include stakeholders from all segments of society.

Another set of initiatives promote the grouping of rural municipalities in order to create a critical mass for development. Italy paved the way with its successful "Territorial Pacts" initiative. These agreements stimulate and co-ordinate investments between private enterprises and local administrations. A similar initiative is being pursued in Mexico where micro-regions provide a framework for infrastructure investment in regional hubs. France has used the concept of "Pays", or areas with distinctive and marketable regional characteristics to promote co-operation among small rural municipalities. The EU LEADER initiative has undeniably contributed to the shaping of a positive self-image in many rural communities, essential to economic renewal and a demographic turnaround. Moreover, it has promoted networking to encourage and facilitate rural areas in their ability learn from each other's experience. This idea of learning from one another is a lesson that the OECD strongly supports and a basic premise of the organization's work.

Co-ordination between levels of government is becoming more flexible. Hierarchical command structures are being replaced by mechanisms that are more responsive to local conditions and local preferences. Flexibility is a strategic advantage and the "contracts" between French regions and the central government are a good example of this. These contracts are the result of a negotiation between the main actors and they define objectives that are relevant for the region and show how different national and local actions, and resources, will contribute to achieving these objectives. This contract-based co-ordination between the central government and the regions is complemented by a similar arrangement between the regions and local authorities.

Lastly, inter-ministerial co-ordination is being reinforced in order to take better account of the impact of different policies on rural areas and to avoid wasteful overlapping. The concept of the "rural lens" has emerged in some countries such as Canada and the United Kingdom as a means to ensure that sectoral ministries are aware, ex ante, of the impact that their policies will have on rural concerns.

Finally, the significance of a new approach to rural policy the emphasis it places on entrepreneurship and initiative, not only on the part of local firms, but also on the part of the public sector. A general pattern seems to be emerging. National authorities set the framework, guidelines or incentives and supply the initial financing, like seed capital for new ventures. The local level defines its strategy, bringing the main actors together for the common goals and projects to be achieved over a given period of time. In a way, this is the essence of decentralization, another issue at the top of the policy agenda in many countries. More than a simple transfer of decision-making powers, decentralisation is the allocation of responsibilities to the level at which implementation will be most cost-effective and, in the process, builds local capacity and initiative.

The OECD, through its work on territorial development and its role as a forum for the exchange of views and innovative practices, will continue to help member and non-member countries enhance the competitiveness of their rural areas and improve the prospects and quality of life for rural citizens.

Thinking Regionally in a Globalizing Economy
by Alan Greenspan

Chairman
Federal Reserve Bank
United States of America

As in all societies, the history of rural America is the history of agriculture. From 1785 through 1935, when all federal lands were withdrawn from settlement, the states or the federal government offered land from $1 to $2 per acre. Indeed, the Homestead Act of 1862 offered 160 acres of federal land in the American Midwest for only a $10 filing fee and an agreement to cultivate the land for five years. Although crop productions increased dramatically as the Great Plains were settled, the abundance of cheap land offered little incentive to cultivate the land intensively. Consequently, apart from fluctuations related to weather, crop yields not surprisingly remained remarkably stable. National average yields for corn were roughly twenty-five bushels per acre from the Civil War to around 1940. Wheat yields during the same three-quarters of a century seldom exceeded fifteen bushels per acre.

The end of the era of cheap land created incentives for intensive cultivation. Partly as a consequence, great waves of innovation and invention swept across American agriculture beginning just before World War II. Discoveries in the use of chemicals helped improve plant nutrition and pest control, and the introduction of new crop varieties, such as hybrid corn, boosted yield potential enormously. The average yield per acre of corn, for example, which was about twenty-five bushels in 1940, increased to more than 100 bushels per acre by the latter 1970s, and this past year, to more than 140 bushels per acre. Yields on wheat, soy beans, cotton, and even hay show similar but somewhat lesser gains. The development of the tractor, the combine, and a host of other farm implements helped intensify cultivation by enabling one farmer to do the work formerly done by ten farmers three quarters of a century earlier and by dispensing with the need to maintain a stable of draft animals that had to be fed and tended.

The rapid gains in farm productivity in the United States continue to this day and along myriad fronts. In agriculture, as everywhere else in our economy, the computer is coming into wider use, as are other new electronic and communications devices. For example, combinations of electronic sensors, computers, and global positioning equipment offer producers extraordinary precision in the application of fertilizers, pesticides, herbicides, and seeds. Not only do these technologies offer lower-cost production to farmers, they also tend to reduce total chemical use and runoff into streams or volatilization into the atmosphere.

Advances in genetics have made available varieties of crops that incorporate a naturally occurring deterrent to insects and thus require few or no pesticide applications. Other work in genetics has produced plant varieties that are resistant to certain herbicides, allowing farmers to reduce tillage and petroleum usage dramatically. A lengthy debate about the long-term healthfulness of these products has been ongoing. Irrespective of the outcome of that debate, the knowledge gained regarding the genome of the main crops should help accelerate plant breeding that underlies the increases in yields of the past six decades. Geneticists, for example, now have the ability to breed varieties of rice that contain vitamin A, which tends to be chronically deficient in countries where rice is a staple.

The gains in productivity have not been limited to crops--livestock productivity has also increased. On average over the past few years, the nation has a smaller cattle herd than it did three decades ago, but beef production has risen more than 20%. The dairy herd is about three-fourths the size that it was in the late 1960s, but the output of milk has increased more than one-third. In the poultry business, the flock of hens has changed little, on net, but the poundage of broilers delivered to retail has risen spectacularly. Pork production in 2003 was up about 50% from three decades ago, even though the inventory of hogs and pigs on the nation's farms was up only slightly. Over time, livestock producers have been exerting ever greater control at all stages of production and have been able to adapt some industrial methods to animal husbandry. In addition, a good part of the increased livestock productivity has come from increased attention to the genetic traits of animals, and these improvements are likely to accelerate with the rapid application of the recent advances in genomics to the livestock sector.

Other avenues of increasing productivity include greater knowledge of the most cost-effective practices regarding cultivation. Here I include the increased use of rotational grazing of livestock to improve rangeland quality and utilization. Reduced or no-tillage crop production techniques continue to gain in popularity, and ways to increase output with these modes of production continue to be found. Also, entomologists maintain active research programs on the use of natural predators for many insect pests.

Overall productivity gains in the United States following World War I reflected the ongoing shift of our workforce from farms, where the level of output per hour was low, to rapidly expanding high-value-added manufacturing. But with cheap farm land rapidly dwindling after 1935, intensive cultivation accelerated, increasing earnings per acre that were rapidly capitalized into land values. The value per acre of farm land adjusted for inflation has tripled since 1940.

But as land values have risen, intensive cultivation is also rapidly closing the gap between productivity on farms and ranches and productivity of non-farm business establishments. Indeed, over the past half-century, agricultural productivity rose at an annual rate of 5%, more than twice the rate for non-farm business firms.

The surge in farm productivity has had profound implications for the size of the farm population and the structure of rural communities. The sharp rise in output per worker created excess supplies of agricultural labour and led to a huge migration of farmers and farm workers from agriculture to other industries, generally in urban areas. The farm population in the United States peaked at 33 million in 1916, held stable through the 1940s, but declined thereafter. Today only a few million people live on farms. Moreover, as rural workers declined in number, some of the smaller villages and trade centres that had formed when earlier, more labour-intensive technologies prevailed were no longer viable as commercial centres. In addition, declining farm populations in some communities in the Great Plains strained social institutions such as schools, county services, and hospitals that tend to require a "critical mass" of population to operate effectively.

Despite the migration of farm populations towards cities, the non-farm population and the level of employment in rural America as a whole have increased substantially over time and have more than offset the declines in populations involved in farming and other resource-based industries. After World War II, growth in manufacturing created many jobs in rural areas, and more recently, many rural places have become home to service-based industries. For all counties that are labelled non-metropolitan by current definitions, the population is about one-fourth larger than it was in 1960, and that finding does not take into account the very rapid growth in counties that were rural in 1960 but have since become part of expanding metropolitan areas. Recent surveys by the Department of Agriculture show rapid population gains in communities close to metropolitan areas, but strong growth has also occurred in many other rural areas, especially those with attractive lifestyles and other amenities that are much in demand among today's workers.

The growing tendency of workers today to migrate to rural areas also reflects space-reducing innovations in transportation, infrastructure, and communications, such as satellite television, that have helped to lessen the physical remoteness of many rural places.

What does this brief sketch of American agricultural history imply about global agricultural development? First, many of the countries where agricultural output is growing most rapidly still report yields that are considerably below those in the United States. For instance, according to Agriculture Department estimates, since the mid-1990s, yields per acre of corn in Argentina have been roughly one-third less than those in the United States, and in China they have been about one-half. Such lower yields suggest that these countries have yet to implement fully the intensive cultivation technologies available to today's farmers and instead depend on a relatively higher input of land and labour. However, average yields in these countries are advancing rapidly, and we can reasonably expect that, just as in the United States, higher farm returns should come along with the yield improvements.

A second vital feature in the development of American agriculture was the importance of unfettered trade. Of course, initially much of the exchange of agricultural commodities occurred within the United States, but as output expanded, exports became increasingly important. Today, our nation's farmers are highly dependent on exports to absorb their remarkable productivity, and their ability to compete internationally depends on lowering unit costs faster than producers in other countries are lowering costs. Given the institutions that our nation has developed for maintaining rapid agricultural innovation and for quickly disseminating the new techniques through the farm economy, U.S. producers are well positioned in this regard. However, foreign producers are adopting farming innovations rapidly as well, and efforts to increase the openness of world markets will need to be maintained and intensified so that the full benefits of farm productivity gains can raise standards of living worldwide.

The phenomenal gains in U.S. agricultural productivity of the past century brought profound benefits to all consumers, regardless of their connection to a farm, in the form of lower prices, better quality, and more choices at retail outlets. But those gains also have been associated with dislocations in many rural areas, largely in the form of a migration of farm workers to more urban areas and the resulting eclipse of many small towns and villages. Although dislocations are bound to accompany economic growth, we should rise to the challenges that come with innovation because innovation brings great improvements in material well-being.

Going forward subsidization in agricultural and rural areas may well be the most crucial question with respect to policies in rural area development. We tend to think of subsidies as a one shot endeavour to improve rates of return on agricultural activity. However, it is very important to remember that once subsidies have been implemented and continue to exist on an ongoing basis the value of the land begins to capitalize on the subsidies. And once subsidies begin to capitalize on the land you begin to create a distortion in the structure of the use of the land and it then becomes exceptionally difficult to unwind the subsidies. It is important to note that subsidies are not granted and then withdrawn when the political scene and pressures have changed, because if this were done it would run a large degree of unfairness.

When a subsidy is created the individual who owns the land finds that the market value of that land, at that particular point, has gone up as the subsidy has capitalized. But when that land is sold the next purchaser no longer gains the advantage of the subsidy because it is embodied in the value of the land. In the end the purchaser of land is actually paying for the presumed subsidies to be received during the life in which that land is owned by that particular person.

If the subsidies are removed when the first owner who initially gained the benefits has already passed from the scene, to be fair the land should be purchased. Indeed that becomes an exceptionally expensive activity. This suggests that the introduction of subsidies should be carefully considered as the long-term implications are exceptionally negative.

This issue is particularly important when endeavouring to enhance the productivity and the adjustment process of rural areas as they are so dramatically impacted by the sharp worldwide increases in agricultural productivity. These increases have very remarkably reduced the need of labour inputs on our farms, obviously and especially amongst developed nations but increasingly in developing nations as well. If we rigidify our rural areas and prevent adjustments from occurring we freeze in all of the old inefficiencies.

As we learned, especially in the United States but probably increasingly everywhere else in the world, flexibility is of crucial importance in enhancing economic welfare and economic growth. The reason for that is that we are in a rapidly changing dynamic in most areas of the world in ways that we cannot anticipate. Innovation is considered the key word for the change we currently confront but innovation by definition is not anticipated. If you can anticipate an innovation it is no longer an innovation. And when we are dealing such dramatic change the last thing we want to do is to undercut the flexibility of our system to adjust to those changes in a way which benefits us all.

Prosperity and Productivity
by David Sampson

Assistant Secretary
Economic Development Agency
Department of Commerce
United States

The bottom-line for rural development today is about building prosperity through a high and rising standard of living. Productivity and productivity growth are the fundamental drivers of prosperity, and innovation is the key driver of productivity. The economic development focus of OECD nations must support innovation to ensure the millions of people that live in rural communities around the world have the skills to be productive and build prosperity.

It is abundantly clear that economies are not hermetically sealed in artificial boundaries and that the dominant reality of rural development today is that we live in a worldwide marketplace. Worldwide commerce means that rural communities must operate and cooperate with countries and economies around the world.

In May 2004, the U.S. Department of Commerce released its report on Competitiveness in Rural U.S. Regions. This comprehensive study funded by the Economic Development Administration and produced by Professor Michael Porter and the Institute for Strategy and Competitiveness at Harvard Business School is an important step in achieving a contemporary understanding and approach to addressing the economic needs of rural America. Its findings, however, can have affects far beyond rural American communities and can serve to benefit rural development throughout the world.

Professor Porter's research is particularly helpful in outlining some clear strategies for rural regions to be successful by detailing the flaws in the current understanding of rural economies, and dismissing the myth that every rural region is the same. The research also suggests that America's rural regions, not unlike other rural regions around the world, have tremendous potential that past efforts have failed to unlock, and that a fresh and collaborative approach – based on new thinking about regional economies – is needed.

One clear message outlined in this report is that the capacity for regional innovation is often driven by industry "clusters", broad networks of companies, suppliers, service firms, academic institutions, and organizations in related industries that, together, bring new products or services to market.

Clusters significantly enhance the ability of regional economies to build prosperity because they act as incubators for innovation. They possess the primary elements needed to transform ideas into prosperity – universities or research centres that foment new knowledge; companies that transform knowledge into new services or products; suppliers that provide critical components or equipment; and marketing and distribution firms that deliver the product to customers. Regions with successful clusters enjoy higher average wages, productivity, rates of business formation, and innovation.

Likewise, Professor Porter's research indicates that purely rural strategies may be missing an important dimension of rural economic growth. Rural areas are linked to urban areas and distinguishing between rural regions and urban regions may miss identifying economic regions. What one thinks of traditionally as a rural region in fact obtains products and services from, and sells outputs to, adjacent regions. In other words, clusters regularly cross over traditional rural-urban boundaries. Consequently, we can think about developing strategies for rural areas around regional hubs and rural spokes. Professor Porter's research shows that to increase prosperity in rural communities, we need to move away from thinking about purely rural strategies. We need to focus on economic regions in which entire competitive clusters are found and develop rural strategies where activities are linked to urban centres of economic activity.

Even though Professor Porter is an American, many other countries have been on the forefront of adopting his ideas, even to a greater extent than we have done in the United States. Many are familiar with the cluster, and hub and spoke principles of economic development and some countries serve as best practice case scenarios for rural development policies. It is clear that Professor Porter's research is a basis for growing rural economies, creating jobs and raising prosperity throughout rural communities worldwide.

An example of American cluster development can be found in rural Greer, South Carolina, where German auto manufacturer BMW has helped develop an automotive cluster and currently employs 4,700 workers. Equally impressive have been the spin off jobs and investment that have resulted from the manufacturing cluster that has formed, including over $4.6 billion of investment by forty-two tier one and tier two suppliers with over 7,200 employees. Additionally, because of its relationship with state and local officials and higher education institutions, particularly Clemson University, BMW has chosen South Carolina for its Global Center of Excellence for the integration of IT and mechanical systems in cars. Additionally, Clemson is building what will be a world renowned International Center for Automotive Research.

Currently there are discussions underway within the United States regarding jobs and international trade. I spend much of my time travelling around the nation and while visiting communities, questions arise about "outsourcing" or the loss of manufacturing jobs, particularly in rural regions of America. This same discussion is taking place in many countries around the world as they face and struggle with the same challenges. Let's be clear, economic transition points, like the one the United States and many other nations are now experiencing, are always hard for companies, communities and especially workers. The strategies discussed at the conference can serve as a foundation for lifting rural communities out of difficult times and help to create jobs, infuse growth and grow prosperity in worldwide rural communities.

Rural communities throughout the world can grow and prosper, however, they must embrace the fact that the global economy is changing and whether it be through regional economic development, cluster development or some other means, rural communities can be fully engaged into the growing economy of their nations. There is no doubt that change is difficult but by embracing it, discovering new and innovative ways of growing an economy and differentiating one's community on its unique set of assets or ideas, a rural community can prosper in an ever-changing world.

PART II: THE RURAL POLICY LABORATORY

LESSONS FROM AROUND THE GLOBE

New Regional Partnerships in the United States
by Gilbert G. Gonzalez

Acting Under-Secretary
USDA Rural Development
United States

Rural development in America requires analyzing past polices, economic factors affecting rural economies and recognizing the need to create policies that results in new opportunities for economic growth. I am optimistic about the economic future for rural America. There are challenges, but in the midst of these challenges there lies opportunity.

On May 10, 2002, during a conference on the study of rural America hosted by the Federal Reserve Bank of Kansas City, Deputy Secretary Moseley presented a position paper entitled, "How Regions Change the Future of Rural Policy", where he discussed the drivers of change for rural development, what USDA brings to the table, promising new industries and identified some challenges yet to be solved. This position paper, in conjunction with the 2001 unveiling of agriculture and rural policy principles recognizing rural policy and agriculture policy are not the same, have helped lay the groundwork for the current focus at USDA Rural Development.

Rural America is at a crossroads. We recognize that we must be innovative in developing strategies to create economic opportunity. While agriculture once was the sustaining staple in many local economies, it no longer provides the stimulus needed for long term viability. It remains an important element, but it may no longer be the economic driver.

Change has been dramatic in rural America over the past half century. In 1950, there were 2053 agricultural dependent counties in the United States. Moving forward a half century, there were only 258 clustered in the Great Plains, Western Middle West, and the Mississippi Delta, where population losses have been greatest. Of the 60 million people who live in rural areas only 2 million depend on agriculture, the other 58 million depend on the development of rural policies.

The data reflects two important realities: First, the development challenge affects more than agriculture. Second, the development solutions must be a good deal broader than agriculture. Further, there are two components I believe will lead to successful economic development in rural communities:

- Diversifying their economic base and

- Developing a regional economy.

In support of these two components, America's rural communities will also benefit from the development of local leadership that focuses on facilitating access to high speed telecommunications, workforce development, and access to capital. If a community has neither the critical mass nor the resources to diversify, it is incumbent upon them to look for solutions that may reach beyond their local community, to a more regional approach to economic development.

We constantly hear that it is not wise to place all of our retirement investment in one stock, mutual or saving fund that it is better to diversify to allow us to sustain cyclical financial market fluctuations, the same rule should apply to a community that is looking for long term economic sustainability. The recruitment of commercial investments should be balanced; it should bring stability to the local economy.

What the drivers of change mean for rural development

Let me expand further on the four drivers of change in rural America:

The first driver is the impact technology is having on rural areas.

A *second driver* is the evolution of domestic and export markets.

A *third driver* is the advance in communication and logistic management.

Fourth, and perhaps most importantly, people move to opportunity. While many decry the loss of population in rural areas and question whether it can be reversed, the *reality* is that people *move toward economic opportunity*. When we create opportunities in rural America, reversal in out-migration occurs.

These drivers of change lead to several conclusions about rural development. Successful economic development in rural communities comes through *Regional Development*. If we are to be successful, we must work together. It is difficult for organizations, public and private, to break down their 'stove piping' and increase communication, co-ordination and cooperation across service offerings. But it must be done, and education and training will be crucial in this effort.

Critical Mass is an important element in encouraging private sector investment. To create sustainable economic growth and the development of human capital, critical mass is important to successful economic development. As businesses require access to a range of complementary private and public services; including education, culture, and recreational services, demand for mass and scalability is critical and should not be overlooked in charting a development strategy. In rural areas this typically means a regional approach encompassing the cooperative efforts of several communities.

Technology has opened new ways to define regions as well as to create critical mass and scales. Communities can now be linked in non traditional ways to help achieve the benefits of regionalism. Flexible manufacturing or service production systems linked via technology can provide and support shared input sourcing, production co-ordination, worker training and marketing. A virtual cluster of business activity can achieve many of the advantages of physical clustering. This can largely overcome the isolation of remote business locations while linking firms with suppliers and customers.

Skilled entrepreneurship and a passion for excellence in business product and performance are absolutely essential ingredients in successful development. This will be particularly true in rural development. Any such approach to rural development must include training in entrepreneurship and business management. Moreover, access to ongoing technical and business management, education and work-force training are bedrock essential to supporting rural economic development.

What USDA brings to regional development

At the federal level the USDA has a long and credible history in playing a role in empowering rural people, rural businesses and rural institutions, to adapt to change while being change agents in building new opportunities. It is our vision to assist rural Americans and their communities by creating economic opportunity and improving the quality of life. We, like many others, have a range of programs supporting economic development, and we are working to make access to those programs as transparent as possible.

USDA rural development

The USDA Rural Development organization is essentially a large investment bank with an $86 billion portfolio. Last year alone, over $13 billion was invested in the future of rural America, which will result in creating or saving over 300,000 jobs.

Since 2001, USDA Rural Development has provided over $37 billion in investment financing and assisted with the creation or saving of over 500,000 jobs. As the only federal organization that can essentially build a town from the ground up through investments in infrastructure, homeownership, and job creation through business development, Rural Development is helping rural Americans achieve the American dream. Rural Development is working to increase the competitive advantage in rural communities. To do this we work with federal partners, education and private sector, along with local leaders. An example of this collaboration is the model established in 2002 to support a successful minority homeownership initiative. The goal to increase minority homeownership by 5.5 million minority families by 2010 was aggressive and required unprecedented co-ordination between federal agencies and the private sector. Since announced the initiative in June 2002, the Census estimates an increase of 1.53 million new minority homeowners.

To assist communities USDA Rural Development has initiatives underway in a number of different areas. The organization is helping rural communities diversify their economic base. We are working to increase the flow of capital to increase homeownership and to support the development of small businesses. Projects to maintain, sustain, and rebuild existing community water, sewer, electric and broadband infrastructure are supported. There is also a focus on facilitating the development of high-speed internet access required to enable rural America to compete both domestically and globally.

The Value Added Development Grant program and Renewable Energy and Energy Efficiency System Improvement (9006) programs have since been introduced to further enhance competitiveness and create jobs.

Challenges yet to be resolved

Regional approaches to rural development are essential to the ability of rural communities to survive and thrive. Opportunities to use regionalization and clustering to support sustainable rural development are both promising and uncertain. There are four challenges that must be successfully met to make this a reliable and successful tool to support rural development.

First, regionalization and clustering will require a high level of cooperation with all parties. That is not easy to achieve. One of the most difficult tasks is that of ensuring effective local governance while maintaining information flows across agencies within the USDA and across other departments and agencies in government. Regional rural development may require new structures to bridge these communication and cooperation gaps.

Rural areas are often burdened with multiple layers of government that no longer meet their emerging needs. It will be important to explore ways public sector governance can adapt to the new economic opportunities that become available to rural America. Public institutions and public policy can play a catalytic role in helping market based regions and clusters coalesce in rural America. This may be a new direction in public policy, one that may require new public institution models and alliances, and one that provides the necessary incentives to encourage participation.

Second, private sector firms must be involved in the development process to achieve sustainable progress. They are the entities that create jobs, investing capital and producing goods and services for sale. Non-profit and government entities will need to play a role, as well. The obstacle here will be facilitating creative partnerships among business and these other players while still remaining attentive to the benefits of local equity investment and control.

Finally, mechanisms for tapping private sector capital to support rural development must become more effective. It is time to think creatively about how venture capital can be better harnessed to address development opportunities in rural America.

On several levels, the USDA is positioned to fill an important catalytic and support role in rural development where its programs can provide support to regional approaches in rural economic development, where that is the decision of the grassroots stakeholders. Constructive and thoughtful engagement by all stakeholders, including businesses and creative government alliances and non profit organizations, is also needed for communities and regions to build on the emerging opportunities.

There are numerous advantages for doing business in rural America. Rural communities can be competitive in recruiting businesses to make commercial investments based on physical infrastructure, economic infrastructure and quality of life.

Commercial investment has been thriving across rural America. According to Conway Data, Inc.'s new plant database, from 2000-2002 the 134 most successful U.S. small towns hosted a total of 1,500 business start-ups or expansions. Success in these communities is based on a multitude of factors, from ranging successfully leveraging existing resources and geographic proximity to transportation modes, to skilled workforce, capital and other factors.

Incentives to increase private investments in rural areas

If the community can market their assets, combine or leverage their resources, and establish local leadership to drive their efforts, they can bring new opportunities to their community. To then meet these demands communities must partner with institutions, both private and public, to bring a complimentary array of resources to bear that will help build the community's capacity to attract and retain commercial enterprises.

To support the increase in economic investments in rural America, USDA Rural Development is implementing two important business investment programs: Rural Business Investment Program and a low documentation business and industry guarantee loan program.

Rural America has many opportunities to not only survive, but to thrive. However to meet these challenges governance must begin at the local level. USDA Rural Development is firmly committed to the future of rural communities, and it is our desire to work in partnership with other federal agencies, and private and public organizations to support a strong economy and create a brighter future for rural America.

Rural Entrepreneurship: A Cooperative Case Study
by Bob Militello

Director
National Grape Cooperative Association, Inc. & Welch Foods, Inc.

The National Grape Cooperative's strategy for National Grape and Welch's has made it a successful cooperative for over 50 years. There are two aspects of this strategy that have driven the cooperative's success as "grape growers who own a packaged food company": First is the governance structure encourages the partnership of the grape production side of the business with the sales, marketing and manufacturing side of the business. Second is the overarching commitment to meet consumer demand in the marketplace.

At National Grape the focus of the cooperative is to return the best possible value for the member's crop. Over the past 15 years National/Welch's has returned a premium over the cash market for Concord and Niagara grapes of about 15% on a net present value basis. In 2003 that premium reached about 38%. The members receive earnings based on their share of the crop sold.

The cooperative's primary purpose is to serve the economic interests of its members. National members contribute by assisting in the financing of their cooperative business. Currently twenty-one per cent of member proceeds are paid in the form of taxable, non-interest bearing twenty-year Allocation Credits (AC) and Permanent Equity Credits (PEC). AC's are currently revolved in six years and one month from issue. They are traded and the last series issued in January 2004 traded at sixty-six and three-fourths per cent of face value. The members are required to maintain a Permanent Equity Credit (PEC) in the amount of fifty dollars per ton based on their floating five-year average crop.

Birth of the cooperative

National Grape was formed when a prominent New York entrepreneur by the name of Jack Kaplan acquired a small grape processing plant in Brocton, NY and started the National Grape Corporation in 1933. Price controls, put in place by the US Government during WWII to control inflation, affected most industries. Farm cooperatives were exempt and could pass through their prices to the market. Kaplan convinced the growers supplying grapes to his plant to form a cooperative and he would sell them the company to take advantage of this opportunity. The growers agreed and National Grape Cooperative was formed in 1945.

In the same year Kaplan acquired the Welch Grape Juice Company and in the early 50's he provided the opportunity for National to purchase Welch's by providing capital via a revolving fund (Allocation Certificates) and at the same time defined how Welch's was to be governed. The advantage of the purchase was that it provided skilled management to run the company. National members benefit from the results of marketing finished products. Grower/members in return can concentrate on what they do best, growing high quality grapes to produce high quality products. National purchased the Welch's stock in 1956 and paid the mortgage off in three years. The first allocation certificates were redeemed eight years after the first issue. Today Welch's is the world leader in the sales and marketing of Concord and Niagara Products.

National Grape and Welch's are two separate cooperatives each with their own board of directors. The National Grape Board is made up of thirteen grape growers who are all members of National Grape and elected by the National Grape membership. The National Grape Board in turn employs a General Manager. National's mission is to provide a reliable market and maximum proceeds for its patrons.

The National Grape Board elects the Welch's Board annually. The Welch's Board is comprised of four National Grape Directors, two Welch's Management Executives (CEO and CFO), and four outside Directors. Outside directors are selected based on their competency in a field important to the Welch mission. Currently, these directors are individuals who have held or currently hold positions of CEO or CFO of successful packaged goods companies – like Nabisco, Bose Corporation and Gorton's Seafood.

The National Grape Board President is elected by the National Grape Board and is also Chairman of the Welch's Board. There is a close working relationship between the National Grape General Manager and the Welch's President.

Welch's mission is in three parts:

- Provide a secure market for member's quality grapes.

- Earn more for the grapes they receive.

- Increase the consumer demand for Concord and Niagara grapes. This part of Welch's mission is by far the most important because it makes the first two parts achievable.

Most agriculture cooperatives, as a rule, have as their board of director's farmers elected by the membership to represent the members. While this may be very democratic, National Grape feels it has developed an approach better suited to its need for strategic guidance and discipline as a consumer packaged-goods company. The cooperative's farmers are not expected to be packaged goods experts or marketers. With the current approach farmers are able to focus on the areas in which they excel, specifically in the art and science of growing grapes. The areas of advertising, packaging, new product development and marketing are left to those with experience in the field.

In selling Welch's to National, Jack Kaplan was relying on the future success of Welch's to pay him for the acquisition. He insisted, and convinced the growers to establish this unique governance system, modelled after public companies. The concern was for the success of Welch's as a packaged goods company – an objective shared by both the growers and the previous owner – Jack Kaplan.

To the Welch's Board of Directors, the growers are the company's stockholders. Board members are elected by the stockholders (National) to ensure the success of the total enterprise, from the farm to the consumer. This partnership, with National growing and providing the grapes and Welch's developing, manufacturing and marketing the products, has experienced remarkable success for over fifty years.

Solid brand = solid demand

Welch's is fully prepared to receive all of the members' quality grapes every year and sell the entire harvest at a significant price premium to the cash market. Welch's is able to meet this task without depressing earnings or creating surpluses, by increasing demand for the growers' grapes and increasing the proceeds on that production through branding.

Welch's has over a century of experience in growing, processing and marketing the Concord grape. The Concord grape was developed in 1853 from the wild fox grape by an amateur plant breeder by the name of Ephraim Bull. The Concord grape is named for the town where it was developed, Welch's hometown, Concord, Massachusetts. Then in 1869, Dr Thomas Welch, relying on the scientific discoveries of Louis Pasteur, pioneered the heat treatment and shelf-stable processing of grape juice - using the Concord grape. National's acquisition of Welch's more than 70 years later included the rights to the processing, manufacturing and marketing knowledge as well as the brand name, all serving as the basis for the partnership enjoyed today. It is through "branding" that the cooperative is able to "add [additional] value" to each case of Concord and National grapes, and accomplish Welch's mission.

Dr. Welch realized this over 134 years ago. It was true then and it is true today. While the strategy "adding value through branding" may seem simple, it is the successful execution of that strategy that is the challenge. Branding is not something that can be accomplished overnight. Branding requires incredible discipline, building a reputation and developing a personality.

Daniel Dillon, Welch's CEO likes to define branding as creating an ethos – "ethos is the distinguishing characteristics, attributes, habits and beliefs of an individual or company". Just as a person establishes an ethos, a personality and a reputation in life, companies do too. When we hear brand names we can easily make a mental picture that we associate to their different, unique ethos. Welch's too creates a mental image in the consumer's mind. It takes many years and the expenditure of hundreds of millions of dollars to create an image for a company and its products, making branding an incredible investment.

A consumer packaged-goods company's success relies upon building and maintaining a brand image. For consumers the Welch's brand stands for excellent, consistent quality in fruit-based products – primarily juices, jams and preserves and primarily grape-based products. Welch's has also made investments in health and nutrition to build demand for grape products.

Dr. Welch in the 1860's instinctively recognized that grape juice was good for you. By the end of the century, Welch's was advertising the healthy goodness of Concord Grape Juice. But those claims were based more on folklore than science. Then in the 1980's the company began to consider the ideas expounded in the The French Paradox, which hypothesized that French men were able to maintain lower cholesterol despite a relatively high fat diet because their per capita consumption of red wines was greater than other populations.

This was a very intriguing claim in that if red wine was able to reduce cholesterol, then purple grape juice might have the same properties. Beginning in 1991, Welch's began sponsoring a number of medical research studies on Concord grape juice. By 1996, results were being made known. Since then, a number of confirming studies have been completed.

Research results have shown that Concord grape juice has more antioxidants and more poly-phenols than comparable juices or even red wine. These properties have been shown to make blood less sticky so it doesn't clog arteries as easily, reduces cholesterol, relaxes the arteries so blood flows more freely and reduces blood pressure. The brand building potential is in publicizing these scientific findings, both through public relations efforts and commercials. All together Welch's, as a $700 million company, spends over $100 million a year advertising, researching, test marketing, developing new packaging, new flavour combinations, promoting the Welch's brand.

In summary, the governance structure of National/Welch has helped to balance the needs of the production side of the business with the sales, marketing and manufacturing side. It has allowed us to stay focused on the important tasks of building and maintaining our brand and increasing the demand for Concord & Niagara grape food products.

The Micro-Region Strategy in Mexico
by Antonio Sánchez Díaz de Rivera

Vice-Minister
Ministry of Social Development
Mexico

Rural areas, many of them characterized by their isolation, scarce and disperse population, high dependence on governmental subsidies and chronic stagnation, pose a major challenge to both central and local governments in most OECD countries. Mexico is no exception. Globalization and free trade opens a whole world of opportunities for everyone, particularly for those countries and regions who have well established competitive advantages.

However the effect of globalization on different regions within nations has been uneven. Rural areas, whose economies have depended heavily on agriculture, have not been able to benefit at the same rate as urban areas. The competition among regions for attracting and retaining investments that support a sustainable development is sharper. This scenario demands from central policy makers, regional and local authorities, a co-ordinated and creative attitude to develop new policy tools capable of capturing the diversity of rural areas and exploiting new opportunities.

Rural development has to be integrated and should not be limited to the agricultural perspective. It should consider the entire regional potential including the natural and cultural richness. The end goal has to be the improvement of the quality of life of the citizens.

It is in this context that the Mexican Federal Government launched the Micro-Region Strategy, a flexible tool designed to speed up the implementation of regional competitiveness, adapt to the new conditions posed by globalization, and provide a prompt response to the challenge of building a self sustainable economy in rural regions. The strategy represents a breakaway from traditional sectorial policies and in its place proposes an integrated bottom-up approach that acknowledges the importance of sharing the responsibility of promoting development with all the social actors involving the efforts of 14 federal ministries, regional and local governments. It puts a particular emphasis on working with local civil society in order to build a strong social capital which serves as the main input in an endogenous process that supports self sustainable development.

The dispersion of the population and the geographic profile of rural areas demand the grouping of Micro-Regions that share a similar ethnic, cultural and geo-economic identity. We have defined 263 Micro-Regions, each one with 5 municipalities on average. In organizing large numbers of small, isolated villages we created territorial hubs or Strategic Community Centres from natural convergence points within the Micro-Regions.

The conditions of most of the Micro-Regions demand a two-part plan of action:

- The first one focuses on establishing a set of conditions that facilitate economical development and include basic infrastructure, social services such as health, education and communications, putting a particular emphasis on building human and social capital.

- The second centres on establishing Micro-Regional Councils that work with an external Local Development Agency and have access to regional funds. Empirical experience in Mexico demonstrates that examples of economically successful rural regions most often had an external input, provided by NGOs or similar organizations.

Within the Micro-Region strategy in Mexico today some of the challenges and opportunities for rural development are related to capacity building in order to respond to the challenges imposed by the process of decentralization.

In addition we need to enhance and support the work of NGOs and civil organizations to encourage the combination of self sustainable economic projects with entrepreneurship as well as human and social capital building. As noted by the OECD Secretary General, the introduction of innovative communication technologies such as high-speed satellite internet connections in long time lagging communities will also be a powerful training tool. The promotion of agglomeration economies *i.e.* the clustering process, will lead to the development of scale economies, so that the business projects promoted in the Micro-Regions will find true viability and competitiveness on a regional, national and global basis.

Improvement in governance is a major task that needs to be tackled by policy makers. Effective co-ordination at both, federal and local level, demands in many cases a new governmental architecture away from traditional sectorial evaluation of results, towards the appreciation of the overall performances and results achieved in target territories. It is important for the strategy to establish a reference base line that will facilitate the regular evaluation of the progress and the impact of the actions undertaken on grounds of rural development.

Mexico is strongly committed in the development of innovative, place-based policies for rural development. We are looking forward to learning from other's experiences and sharing our own. To this end the Social Development Ministry of Mexico, along with the OECD, will be hosting an international conference on rural development in April 2005 in Oaxaca, Mexico.

Linking Rural Policy and Regional Development in Western Canada
by Oryssia Lennie

Deputy Minister
Western Economic Diversification
Canada

I'd like to give you a sense, very briefly, of what is happening in Canada today in terms of rural initiatives and policies, first from a national perspective and then from a regional rural perspective, turning to my own department, Western Economic Diversification, and its activities in Western Canada.

Similar to rural areas around the world, Canada is experiencing profound changes and has to respond from a policy perspective. But we face some significant challenges in doing so. With 32.2 million people spread over nearly 10 million square kilometres, we're one of the least densely populated countries in the world. Many of our communities are not only rural, but often remote as well. The second key Canadian characteristic is our diversity culturally, linguistically, geographically and economically. It's a factor the Government of Canada must take into account in every initiative it undertakes. A single, uniform approach could never hope to be effective in responding to the vast range of realities that exists from coast to coast to coast.

In the past, rural policies have been largely geared toward agriculture; however "rural" is not synonymous with "agriculture" anymore. Certainly that is the case in Canada.

A year ago, the Canadian Government proposed a new national rural policy framework involving orders of government. The framework is centred on the thesis that the prosperity of rural Canada benefits the whole nation, and that we need to work towards the long-term sustainability and viability of rural communities and provide an environment where people have access to economic and social opportunities to improve their quality of life and self-reliance. The framework identifies three objectives: to support community capacity building, to support community and sector initiatives to improve and renew the rural economic and social basis, and to improve collaboration across and among governments on rural issues. The framework also provides an important "rural lens" through which other federal policies and programs can be reviewed to ensure the needs and priorities of rural Canadians are considered. Meetings are being held between federal, provincial and territorial ministers responsible for rural development, as they work towards the completion and implementation of the rural policy framework.

Investing in rural infrastructure

The renewal and expansion of basic infrastructure is another area where the Government of Canada has made investments in Canadian communities, large and small. Some $12 billion has been invested over the past decade in core public infrastructure projects – water, sewers, roads, flood-protection, cultural and recreational facilities. Our newest commitment in this area is the Municipal Rural Infrastructure Fund. Designed to respond to the needs of smaller municipalities, the Fund will invest a further 1 billion dollars in infrastructure that sustains economic growth and supports an enhanced quality of life in Canada's rural areas.

Technology

Given the remoteness of many Canadian communities, information technology is one of the most important components of rural infrastructure. As noted by the OECD, "the ICT revolution provides rural areas with tremendous opportunity." It's an opportunity we in Canada have been working hard to open up to our rural communities. Canada already ranks as one of the most connected countries in the world. We have made a commitment to provide broadband Internet access for every community – rural, northern, remote and Aboriginal – by the end of 2005.

We have made substantial progress toward this goal and are now reaching into space to bring us even closer. A National Satellite Initiative, announced last September, will expand broadband access to some 400 remote and northern communities where satellite is the only practical means of providing broadband access. Clearly, this is a major investment; however we believe the Internet can be a powerful tool for economic and social development for all Canadians, no matter where or how they live.

References have been made to tele-health, distance learning, e-commerce as just a few of the applications where technology can bridge the distance between communities and make amenities and opportunities more available in rural and remote areas. Hand in hand with this is the electronic delivery of government services or government-on-line, and we're making significant progress in having all Canadians able to access all government information and services on-line at the time and place of their choosing. We have moved beyond the mature delivery stage into service transformation, where e-government ceases to be a separate initiative and becomes part of a wider transformation of service. Canada's success in this area is one we're very proud of, but it has been driven as much by need as by policy. Once technology made it possible to span the geographic immensity of our nation, it became the logical, most efficient method to deliver services to our widely dispersed population.

The social economy

Another concept which is starting to emerge increasingly in Canada is the expansion of the definition of "economy" to include the "social economy" *i.e.* organizations that run like businesses, producing goods and services, but which manage their operations not for profit, but to pursue social, community and environmental goals. In the federal budget delivered on March 23, 2004, the Canadian Government has pledged to support this sector's growing contribution to the vitality of our communities. This will be done by widening the scope of programs currently available to small businesses to include these social enterprises, and by providing new funding for pilot programs designed to strengthen capacity building and financing in this area. The social economy is a powerful force to improve conditions in communities across Canada and we believe that supporting it will become a key part of our policy tool kit.

The West

I represent the regional development department of the Government of Canada, based in Western Canada, representing the four western provinces – British Columbia, Alberta, Saskatchewan and Manitoba. Part of the department's work is to connect western Canadians more closely to the Government of Canada and to give voice in Ottawa to western Canadian rural and urban issues.

Compared with the rest of Canada, the West is considerably more dependant on primary industries. A full 15% of the West's economy is based on our primary sectors, compared with 3% in the rest of Canada. That impact becomes even greater when you consider the many businesses and retail activities, particularly in rural areas, whose fortunes are so closely linked to those of the major natural resource sectors. Adding to this challenge is the fact the rural West has been through some difficult times recently. Devastating events, like forest fires, drought, BSE and avian flu, have sent wave after wave of economic shocks sweeping across the region.

These events have served to reinforce our awareness of the vulnerability that results from resource reliance and our increasingly interlinked global economy. There is a pressing need to diversify our economy and to ensure our rural communities are able to respond to the global realities of the 21st century.

Speakers at this conference discussed the fact that initiatives can't just reach out to rural communities; they have to be resident in the community and they have to be custom-designed by that community. In rural areas in Western Canada, the Western Economic Diversification Department (WD) funds and maintains volunteer-led non-profit organizations called Community Futures Development Corporations (CFDC). Currently there are more than 90 of them across the West. They have as a common goal to build stronger communities by developing local solutions to local challenges.

The CFDC's business development function is to encourage local entrepreneurs and provide them with resources to succeed. They serve as a community-driven economic renewal initiative, helping rural communities develop and implement innovative strategies for dealing with a changing economic environment.

An example of this can be seen in the case of Vancouver Island. Until recently, the economic outlook for the heavily forestry-dependent northern part of the Island was extremely grim. Looking a little deeper into the forest though, the local CFDC found more than just trees. They found an abundance of non-timber forest products – berries, mushrooms, medicinal and pharmaceutical products, cedar oil, and floral greens such as ferns, mosses and cedar boughs. With funding provided by WD, the CFDC partnered with an academic institution and consulted with First Nations and others to create a business plan for the Northern Island Non-Timber Forest Products Innovation Centre. An application has also been made for funding that would make the centre a reality.

The opportunities for diversification are varied as the communities themselves, ranging from diversification of traditional activities to innovative new projects, from value-added agriculture to value-added wood products to tourism. By fostering the development of new products and markets for non-timber forest products, the centre will use the area's existing assets to create new streams of income leading to new employment opportunities. It is a case of seizing the opportunities of globalization using local assets.

Aboriginal inclusion

I cannot talk about rural Western Canada without mentioning our Aboriginal population. Western Canada is home to about 63% of Canada's Aboriginal population. They are one of the fastest growing segments of the Canadian population, with about 50% of the Aboriginal population under 25 years of age.

As a department, WD undertakes several roles. First it works to help Aboriginal people access capital and establish and grow their businesses through an Aboriginal Business Services Network and an on-line business resource centre website. We also work closely with community leaders and industries to support projects designed to help increase the number of Aboriginal people registering for and completing apprenticeship programs. These programs serve a dual purpose by increasing sources of skilled labour and ensuring the benefits from major resource development projects accrue to Aboriginal communities.

Conclusion

I'd like to conclude with a brief summary of the key elements of WD's approach for addressing rural development. It is based on key elements from lessons learned during our seventeen years of working on behalf of Western Canadians. They also align very well with those set out by other speakers at the conference. They are:

- A clear policy framework that sets out federal goals and priorities for rural development and provides a "lens" for assessing the rural impacts and opportunities of government policies

- An emphasis on building community based partnerships and networks that harness local resources and commitment and bring all major government and industry players to the table

- Building a modern physical and electronic infrastructure that links rural areas to major urban, regional, and national centres and economic clusters

- The need for regionally tailored and flexible policies and programs that encourage innovation at the local level and build on the economic, social, environmental, and cultural strengths within rural communities and regions.

The very heart of the Canadian identity is deeply rooted in our rural history. As we become increasingly urbanized, we recognize the need to work together to preserve and enhance this vital component of our shared past and future. Sustainable rural development is a challenge, but we are seeing promise for the future of our rural regions.

Reducing the Territorial Divide in France: Redefining Regions
by Nicolas Jacquet

Délégué
Territorial Planning and Regional Action (DATAR)
France

Recently in the heart of the Massif Central Jacques Chirac, the President of the French Republic denounced the risk of a territorial divide. On one side, France has urban areas that benefit from technical progress, the comfort of employment and established infrastructure. On the side there are rural areas benefiting little from these major changes. DATAR and Mr. Hervé Gaymard, the minister responsible for rural affairs, have been charged to develop a governmental plan to address the needs identified in rural areas.

New stakes for rural France

Based on an analysis of the changes within the rural world decisions were made during the inter-ministerial committee for territorial planning and development (CIADT) on September 3rd 2003 and a Council of Ministers, held the same day, to approve the draft law on the development of rural territories.

Rural is not synonymous with agriculture anymore.

The rural space is first a **space of production** however, its physiognomy is changing. While agricultural activity and forested spaces continue to dominate geographically, their contribution in terms of employment has considerably decreased. Rural areas are now more industrial and blue collar, with on average twice as much industrial employment in rural commuting areas as agricultural and agro-food employment combined. But this is largely residential employment, related to activities linked directly to the needs of the inhabitants, in areas such as private services, education and health services. Today this represents more than 50% of rural employment. Altogether, this production space enjoys a certain degree of growth. In the rural urban periphery growth has been the strongest at 16% between 1990 and 1999, against a national average of 3.5%. Predominantly rural spaces, those situated outside the spheres of urban influence, have experienced a more modest increase of approximately 1%.

Rural space is also a **residential space**. As more people choose to live in rural environments, peripheral urbanisation is increasing. Areas defined as rural municipalities situated at the urban periphery have seen their population increase between 1990 and 1999 (from 8.8 to 12.25 million inhabitants) as well as their area (5000 additional municipalities). Different people are moving to these areas for a variety of reasons. Young retirees seeking to establish their "roots", active people sometimes developing innovative projects, as well as less favoured populations are going to live in rural areas. As a result today the migratory balance for new inhabitants moving to predominantly rural areas is positive (+ 410 000 inhabitants).

Rural space plays **a role in leisure and tourism**. With 320 million overnight stays, and a regular increase in visits, the countryside is frequently a destination location. Rural space is the translation of major expectations, namely the quest for "calm" and "tranquillity". A large part of the recreational activity in rural spaces does not give way to market transactions. Of French citizens who spend their vacation in the countryside 52% declare that they spend their vacation in either a family or a friend's houses, and 26% in vacation homes (9% of households own a second home).

Finally rural space plays **a role in nature**. Four great stakes for our societies are identified today in terms of space and natural environments: the protection of natural resources, the maintenance of bio-diversity, protection against natural catastrophes and the preservation of scenic and quality of living conditions. The present and the future of these stakes are mostly being played in rural territories.

Rural areas are not homogeneous.

In a simplified fashion, one can say that three rural Frances are emerging today.

The **city countryside**, whether peripheral urban with a dominant residential function or dense rural spaces with residential and production functions, is increasing as a percentage of the overall territory. It is at this level that preoccupying conflicts appear in terms of land use (40% of agricultural land is today situated in urban areas of influence). Public policies must propose management tools adapted to these stakes.

The **declining countryside** is defined by low density, mono-activity and a regressive demographic trend. There are two sub-categories the first being *agricultural rural space, ageing and with low density*. This includes less than 500 cantons, with an average density of 23 inhabitants per square kilometre, an older than average aged population and generally modest living conditions. Second we have *the traditional rural worker's space,* marked by the permanent foot-print of an industry such as textiles or metal-works, these areas are mostly concentrated north of the Le Havre-Strasbourg line. One asset in these areas is a substantial population though a typically high level of unemployment (14.3%)

keeps it in a state of fragility. Its demographic decline, one born, raised and dies in the same place, is beginning. In all cases development policies are needed and this concerns the regional as well as the national policies as a whole.

The **new countryside** is that which develops simultaneously, though in different proportions, its residential, tourism and nature functions. Such is the case for the Alps which have benefited from the development of ski resorts, for the Mediterranean coastline (Côte d'Azur) and for the Atlantic coastline. They regroup already close to 300 cantons, a figure that could increase if the intermediate rural areas were to direct their evolution towards multi-functionality. Currently, the physiognomy of these areas does not authorise them to be classified in such a category. These intermediate rural areas represent a group of close to 900 cantons. They also have a diversified physiognomy and public policy must accompany them in their transformation.

The forms of local governance have profoundly evolved.

The institutional framework has dramatically changed. Known for its number of municipalities, more than 36 000, France has lived a period of active inter-municipal restructuring. Today more than 80% of the population lives in a municipality that participates in an EPCI (a public agency for inter-municipal co-operation). But France has also been restructuring "project spaces", or "Pays", regroupings of usually several inter-municipal entities around a development charter which includes a contract between the region and the State. On July 1st 2004, close to 300 boundaries of "Pays" were either under validation or accepted, covering close to 70% of the territory. The Natural Regional Parks are true sustainable development laboratories, as economic development, valuation of heritage and preservation of natural and cultural resources are articulated here. They are experiencing rapid growth: in December 2003 there were 43 such parks, covering close to 13% of the national territory. In addition, the European LEADER programs have made considerable contributions to the practices of local development, with territorial organisation and the utilization of public-private Partnerships now commonplace.

A new ambition for the rural world

The government is working to implement pro-active policy, and at the same time adapt to the diversity of situations confronted by rural territories. Following a battery of actions over the last two years, a draft law and several inter-ministerial committees have been put in place. Priority has been given to the following four points:

- Housing is of critical importance as there is no sustainable development of rural territories without inhabitants. Often it is the availability of quality housing that is missing.

- Economic development should then follow, as the durability of development is linked to the sustainability of activities. Government policy was decidedly differentiated, to face the previously mentioned stakes.

- Services to enterprises and the population.

- Land management.

Developing a housing policy

Housing policies have always been an urban issue, designed to manage concentrated city populations. Now with migratory reversal we must invent a policy for rural housing.

The supply of housing, in particular rental housing, is insufficient both in qualitative and quantitative terms. Currently 700 000 dwellings are still qualified as unliveable and rental housing represents only 27% of the total, as compared to 45% in urban areas. A housing policy for rural areas, since they are diffuse, requires the mobilisation of landlords. However, this presents another challenge in that they have typically modest revenues and thus limited incentive to participate. An important incentive policy is needed to address this need.

Supporting economic development and attractiveness

The government has also taken a number of incentive-based measures in favour of the development of the most fragile rural areas. A set of fiscal measures aimed to sustain activity as well as create conditions conducive to development were put in place. Among others these measures included exemptions for firms from corporate income tax during their first five years of operation and facilitation of the renewal of brownfields, whether from industrial, commercial or traditional activities.

Within the area of development, plural activity is now accepted. It is furthered by the promotion of employers groups, access for seasonal workers to vocational training, the development of shared time between public and private sector jobs, and the simplification of the social security regimes for those engaging simultaneously in several activities.

Guaranteeing quality living conditions and access to services

Maintaining quality services for all is a true challenge. First a change in managerial culture is required, putting the citizen at the heart of the system. The government has recently launched a modernisation program of public services. By employing a multi-functional approach, and by distinguishing what is part of the front office and what belongs to the back-office, the ambition is to offer to users public services adapted to the realities of the 21st century, with multi-purpose services available locally.

Certain domains require specific analysis. In the field of healthcare, the government has taken measures to attract professionals to low density areas that lack medical services. They have done this by concurrently improving the organisation of the healthcare system (establishing links between hospital centres and physicians, creating medical centres), training programs (offering incentives to practice in rural areas during studies) and settlement subsidies (allocating up to 50 000 euros over 5 years).

It is necessary to guarantee the same modernity in access to service for both urban and rural areas. The first action consists in guaranteeing people, small businesses and firms, access to new technologies. The government has pledged to abolish the "digital divide" that significantly affects rural territories and thus has committed that 99% of the population will have mobile telephony coverage by 2007. Concerning broadband, the government has created a support fund for projects carried out by local governments in favour of broadband development, with a current allocation of 100 million euros. In addition the government has taken certain fiscal measures to facilitate the development of all technologies related to broadband (wire, satellite, hi-fi, electric power lines, ADSL…). Finished road, rail and air access constitute another objective.

A certain number of important projects were planned in this field during a recent inter-ministerial committee meeting. A reform of the support system for deficit-running air links has also been undertaken to guarantee access between economic metropolises.

Ensuring sustainable development of spaces

Land management is imperative to the development of economic activities, particularly for agriculture and forestry, and it is gaining new momentum through government guidelines. The preservation of natural spaces and those of the urban periphery is being reinforced through specific planning tools. Land parcel assembly schemes are being totally modernised with a greater concern for environmental matters. Wetlands and pastures, which constitute eco-systems to be preserved, benefit from specific measures such as exemption of fiscal tax burdens for the owners. Also, there has been an effort to find a better balance between hunting rights, an activity which contributes to the development of rural territories, and the preservation of wildlife.

Policy for mountainous areas is another area of focus for government initiatives. The institutions which intervene in "mountain governance" have been reinforced. Mountainous area committees are in the process of establishing schemes for these areas, based on partnerships between the state and local government. Specific measures have been taken into account for the challenges that are present in mountainous regions.

Conclusion

The new impulse given to rural policies is in line with the new direction that will be taken within the EU framework. From this point of view, the reform of common agricultural policy must confirm the important place of rural development. The goal of the French government is to give equal development opportunities to the rural world and to the urban world. It is true that the countryside will always have something extra: quality of life, or, to cite the poet Andrès Bello on freedom: "you like freedom, it lives in the countryside".

Federal Co-ordination in Austria
by Wolf Huber

Director
Co-ordination of Regional Policy and Spatial Planning
Federal Chancellery
Austria

Territorial policies in a federal system: multi-level multi-sector governance

The traditional understanding of public policy-making usually involves a strictly hierarchical structure: one single decision maker, or decision making body on top and subordinate agents implementing the policy. Decisions are taken in the name of a homogenous public interest. The implementation of the policy is co-ordinated by the binding central decision (command) and supervised on the basis of full information (control).

Territorial policies in federal systems, however, do not correspond with this model:

Federal systems may vary considerably in the size and number of regions as well as in the distribution of constitutional powers and budgetary resources between federal (national) and regional (State, Länder, Canton, *etc.*) levels. All of them, however, are characterized by their multi-level character of government and legislation, *i.e.* the existence of autonomous fields of policy making given to the regional level. It might thus be the case that different elements – legal framework, finance, planning and technical implementation – of one specific policy are split among different levels of government. In such fields of regional autonomy central government has no formal power either to directly influence (command) regional government decisions and actions or to hold them responsible for the outcomes of their actions (control).

Policies with a territorial focus, such as rural policy, urban policy, regional policy, etc. are characterized by their multi-sector approach. They may comprise elements of economic, agricultural, environmental, transport, labour-market, education, social, housing or cultural policies. The responsibility for these sectoral policies is usually split among different ministries or departments, each having a certain degree of institutional independence. In Austria, each minister is directly responsible to parliament; the Federal Chancellor (Prime Minister) has no formal right to give directives to other ministers. In a federal system, furthermore, these sectoral policies would most probably be distributed between federal and regional government levels.

Multi-level multi-sector policies therefore have to be co-ordinated without being able to rely on command and control.

Challenges for multi-level and multi-sector governance

Each of the institutions and levels of government involved in multi-level multi-sector policies has its own institutional self-interest, concerning resources and power, as well as specific policy agendas. These policies therefore are characterized by multiple conflicts of interest and competing agendas within the public sphere, not only between policies but even within one specific policy.

The situation is further aggravated by the fact that different public sectors are dominated by different professional languages, logics, views and values. What seems crucial to economists often seems irrelevant to spatial planners, and vice-versa. And what might appear to be a solution for a problem to agricultural experts or transport planners might create a new problem from the perspective of an environmental authority, and vice-versa.

Sometimes financial tools, such as conditional grants that act as a "golden rein", are used to retain or introduce a certain element of command & control, to establish dependence for formally autonomous partners. But such financial tools are not always available. And if they are available they do not always render the desired results, because "command" is confused by conflicting objectives and "control" is jeopardized by the impossibility of getting sufficient information on highly complex and dynamic phenomena.

This raises the fundamental question of multi-level and multi-sector governance: Is it possible? And if so, how? The major challenge lays in co-ordinating a multitude of autonomous agents with different, often competing, interests, agendas and views. This must be done without formal power or actual possibility to force others into acting according to one's own agenda and without full information, *i.e.* beyond the traditional co-ordination model of command and control.

This question, by the way, is not new to people familiar with territorial development policies. Development has always been heavily dependent on open-minded attitudes and innovative behaviour of private agents, which has to be stimulated and encouraged by softer forms of intervention, not forcibly by command and control.

According to my experience multi-level multi-sector co-ordination is possible, but not to the extent promised by traditional planning theories and not in the traditional way.

There are institutional arrangements for co-ordination, which are suited to facilitate multi-level multi-sector policy making, to render the desired outcomes of complex territorial policies at least more likely.

Co-ordination as service

Co-ordinators usually are confronted with great scepticism among those they want to co-ordinate, particularly as they are afraid to have their autonomy reduced. Any attempt of co-ordinators to adopt an inappropriate attitude of dominance will increase resistance and make successful co-ordination less likely.

Acceptance for the concerns of the co-ordinator, however, will rise among those being co-ordinated if they benefit from the co-ordination. They will be open to this support if they are provided with better information on relevant procedures or innovative solution proposals relevant to their policies, if they are supported in their attempts to raise public awareness for their agenda or if the co-ordinator succeeds in mediating conflicts. Consequently co-ordinators, rather than command, need to be ready to listen. For multi-sector policies co-ordinators have to be familiar with the different professional languages, values and views involved, and able to "translate" a message from one logic to another. Co-ordinators should act as honest brokers and remain impartial in conflicts (concerning both institutional interest or policy objectives) between institutions involved.

The services of co-ordinators have to be marketed to increase awareness of the benefits of cooperation. This requires knowledge of the demand side, in other words a good co-ordinator has to know how the world looks like from the perspective of those he wants to co-ordinate.

The existence of an external challenge (a "common enemy"), or a clear win-win situation make the benefits of co-ordinated action more obvious. Financial incentives, which do not have to be very high, can compensate for additional transaction costs and thus reduce barriers to cooperation.

Impartial institutions specialized in co-ordination

Different autonomous agents of similar political or economic power with their own strong interests and policy objectives will often find it difficult to accept anyone from among themselves as a co-ordinator. This is for good reason as people with a strong commitment to their own agenda usually have difficulties adopting an impartial, or rather all-partial, role as an honest broker and neutral co-ordinator. This problem can be overcome by creating special institutions for co-ordination. My position co-ordinating regional policy in Austria for example has proved to be much easier being located in the Federal Chancellery (Prime Ministers office, formally in charge of government co-ordination) than in the 1980s when we were located in a sectoral ministry.

For the purposes of multi-level multi-sector policy co-ordination the creation of separate intermediary institutions (*e.g.* regional development associations, territorial employment pacts) has proved to be successful in Austria and many other countries. To compensate for the lack of formal co-ordination tools in the Austrian federal system, the Austrian Conference on Spatial Planning (ÖROK) was established in 1971. It was designed to serve as a common platform for all federal ministries, regional governments, representatives of local government associations and social partners to deal with multi-level multi-sector issues of spatial and regional development policies. After accession to the European Union this well-accepted co-ordination platform has also been used successfully for the co-ordination of EU structural policies in Austria. In spite of a very fragmented institutional framework for regional policies this co-ordination platform has enabled us to implement the extremely complicated EU structural policies rather successfully.

Communication in informal networks

Efficient and effective co-ordination of dynamic processes, outlined in complex policies, requires quick transfer of high quantities of information. Traditional formal exchange of information along hierarchical communication chains, typical for bureaucratic systems, has proved to be highly inadequate for this requirement as formal processes of information transfer are much too slow. Serious bottlenecks are created by the limited capacity of positions at the top of the hierarchy to process information. In order to cope with the challenge of information it has proved to be more appropriate to use informal, non-hierarchical networks among competent people working at different levels of administrative and political hierarchies.

Informal communication has one important prerequisite: trust. Trust requires a certain degree of stability in personal relations and framework conditions and, above all, the positive experience shared by all network partners, that cooperation renders a positive value-added for all participants. According to my experience it is a task of crucial strategic importance for multi-level multi-sector policies to establish such cooperation networks and create an atmosphere of mutual trust. The above mentioned intermediary institutions in Austria (ÖROK, Regional development associations), are using informal communication networks in most of their everyday work and are good examples of the effectiveness and efficiency of this type of communication.

Patience and flexibility

Time is crucial for successful co-ordination in many ways. Processes like information generation, processing and transfer, learning or negotiations to solve conflicts require time, usually much more than expected. This requirement seriously limits the quantity of co-ordination work that can be managed with a given working capacity. The traditional expectation that everything should be co-ordinated with everything therefore remains an illusion. A successful co-ordinator has to make decisions on priorities.

Innovations, which imply changes in people's attitudes and behaviour, require even more time. Patience therefore is a necessary attribute of a good co-ordinator who wants to avoid frustration. If innovation occurs, however, it does so often without warning, *e.g.* when the right people meet at the right time at the right place. A good co-ordinator should be able to recognize such "windows of opportunity" as early as possible and have sufficient flexibility to react without delay.

A new approach to policy making

It should have become obvious that the type of policy co-ordination described above implies a completely different understanding of policy making: A "policy" is not any longer a static set of public activities defined ex-ante, implemented mechanically in a linear and hierarchic structure and controlled ex-post. Rather it should be seen as an emergent dynamic phenomenon of creating and gradually modifying a joint understanding of the "what", "why" and "how" of certain public activities in an on-going communication process. Based largely on trial and error, this process reflects past results, monitors on-going activities and develops new perspectives for future activities.

Central government co-ordination aims at organizing this policy process to keep it fluent and innovative and to increase the adaptability of the whole process of economic and social development.

The Living Countryside in the Netherlands
by Kees de Ruiter

Director
Department of Rural Policy
Ministry of Agriculture, Nature and Food Quality
The Netherlands

Holland is a small country with a dense population of 16 million inhabitants. The rural areas face a lot of problems, partly related to this urban pressure. First we have to deal with major changes in the European policy for agriculture and the liberalisation of the world market. This will be increasingly challenging as the price of land is high and it will be very difficult to realize competitive and sustainable agriculture in the future. This will invariably have significant consequences for the typical Dutch landscape, made up of farmers and needing farming to preserve it.

In the second place, we have to deal with water. The sea level is coming up, land is going down and the Western part of the Netherlands is drowning. In Holland we will have to accept the guidance of water instead of fighting it, a sort of cultural-revolution in the Netherlands. Besides this problem with quantity, we also have a problem with quality. In order to achieve European objectives the use of land should be less dense making the reality for agriculture even more challenging.

In the third place, we have to deal with the pressure of recreation and leisure. Approximately 16 million people occupy the countryside with, among other things, second homes, horse farms and footpath activity. This means opportunities from an economic perspective but it also threatens the qualities people are looking for, namely silence and beauty.

We have a lot of experiences with regional approaches. Together with other stakeholders we are working to develop plans for a living countryside in the future. These experiences have lead to a set of recommendations:

1. Plans should be tailor-made and bottom-up, encouraging creativity and innovation. In an effort to involve the maximum number of players it is vital to also allow some space for controversial activities. These will serve as inspiration for others to develop solutions to address problems and leverage opportunities.

2. Ideas must be followed up with clear-cut implementation plans. This not only maximizes the impact of the solution but it also demonstrates a serious level of commitment for success.

3. Planning stage should be extended when necessary to ensure that the solution accurately and efficiently addresses the problem or opportunity. In the countryside planning is cumbersome; however decisions should not be made to minimize objections.

4. Social and social-cultural impacts need to be a central focus. The countryside is more than farming and nature; it is also a place of history, language, music and small communities.

5. A balance must be struck between people (cultural, leisure), planet (nature and environment) and profit (farming, tourism).

6. Regional planning should be approached a bit as a trial and error exercise. While blueprints may be comforting, there is no set success model for all regions.

As stated in a very popular quote from the Netherlands, happiness is a direction and not a destination.

Rural development in Europe: Approaches and Future Perspectives
by Francesco Mantino

Head of the Research Unit
Rural Development and Structural Policies
National Institute for Agricultural Economics
Italy

Introduction

Rural industries are an integral part of local development in rural areas. I prefer to use the notion of local development instead of rural development, as it is so widely used in European terminology. Local development is a very difficult task to accomplish through public policy, namely because it requires a long list of "ingredients", such as:

1. Supporting *structural change* in agriculture;

2. Developing opportunities for *income diversification* for the active rural population in other sectors;

3. Creating favourable conditions for *internal and external investments* (endogenous and exogenous flows of investment in rural activities);

4. Encouraging increased *linkages* among different sectors;

5. Enhancing *living conditions* for local populations.

Such "ingredients" represent the main objectives typically assumed by public programmes of rural development. But local development in rural areas is not only a mere aggregation of these "ingredients". Since the seventies many Italian economists and sociologists have focused their research on various cases of local development and territorial differentiation. Following these research efforts Italian local development has evolved in a number of different ways: clusters, industrial districts, local systems and "filieres". Pioneers in these fields of study are well-known researchers such as Beccattini (2000), Bagnasco (1977, 2003) and Garofoli (1991, 2003). Some implementation of these policies in rural areas, with references to Italian cases, can be found in Iacoponi (1990). A short survey of these applications has also been developed by Mantino (1995).

Studies of Italian cases have shown that local development depends on many other "ingredients". Historical factors are particularly important in local development as it is a cumulative process where pre-existing structural and cultural factors influence the nature and the direction of the development process. Social capital, as the combination of skills, social networks, trust, cultural attitudes and values, is another considerable force. Innovation also plays a key role, especially through the generation and transfer of it within territories and from outside. Another major element is local institutions, ranging from public and private structures of governance to "capacity building" of policy actors and local partnerships.

All these "ingredients" add to the complexity of the models of local development with each area following its own pattern for local development. The role of policies in facilitating or promoting local development depends upon the institutional and social "ability" of economic and social actors to utilize available policies. The level of commitment to the policies implemented plays a major role in the level of impact as does the efficiency of the delivery system. The nature of the chosen policy approach, integrated or sectoral, is another factor that can dramatically increase complexity.

The effectiveness of local development policies depends on a combination of the local "ingredients", and on the nature of policies directed to local areas. The nature of the policies implemented is particularly important when identifying the types of incentives and their combination.

The main questions which this paper intends to develop are the following:

- To what extent has EU rural development policy (RDP) incorporated these "ingredients" in designing programmes for the EU-15 Member States?

- Which concrete strategies are pursued by EU Member States in their RDP programmes and what driving forces influence the actual objectives of these programmes?

- What is the role of institutions in enhancing the quality of RDP programmes (in terms of effectiveness), particularly those institutions involved in the delivery system (national, regional or local)?

The EU rural development policies (RDP) throughout 2000-2006: programmes, objectives and strategies

EU rural development policies have a number of fundamental rules and elements. National or regional programmes are prepared by Member States/Regions on a multi-annual base, usually for seven years. All programmes are co-financed by EU, Member States and Regions with common rules for programming, implementing, monitoring, evaluating and financial control. The types of interventions, or measures, are pre-defined by EU regulations. This results in a "menu approach", where Member States/Regions choose main dishes and then adapt them to their needs. Constraints are typically linked either to financial resources (the EU allocates to Member States who in turn allocate funds among Regions) and rules of implementation (sectoral restrictions, required detailed financial plans, limitations in financial plan modification, top-down criteria for selecting beneficiaries, etc.).

There is a distinct separation of rural development plans from regional development policies. The only exception is in lagging regions, also known as Objective 1 regions, where rural areas are included in regional development programmes following the principle of integration. The LEADER (*liason entre actions de development rural*) programme is another rural programme comprised of pilot and innovative interventions implemented through local partnerships in territories with fewer than 100 000 inhabitants, though currently only with limited funding. Global resources devoted to rural development in Europe are 49.2 billions euros, including only the EU co-financing, with most of the resources directed to lagging regions.

Rural development policies are an assorted mix of old and new tools. The more traditional tools are those derived from the classical structural policy introduced in the early seventies by the European Community. The main types of interventions that belong to the classical structural policy are farm investments supports, incentives for agro-food industry and income support to farmers operating in disadvantaged areas. Then in 1992, a reform of the agricultural policy promoted by Commissioner McSharry introduced new measures aimed at accompanying the reduction of farm support, modernising the agricultural sector and driving it towards more environmentally orientated practices. The McSharry reform introduced an important group of measures, called the "accompanying measures" of the 1992 reform process: early retirement, agro-environment, re-forestation of agricultural land. All provide direct aid to farm income without a specific link to an investment project. Their specific objectives are different in that respectively they tend to offer an incentive for elder family members to retire, the implementation of environmentally sustainable farm practises and the reduction of agricultural-use land. The more recent measures introduced in the EU toolbox are those devoted to the support of the rural territories and farm diversification. This group includes different types of measures, *i.e.* support of irrigation investments, services for farm and rural populations, and craft and tourism activity in rural areas, etc. These measures correspond more to the new vision of rural development that is taking place in the EU language and regulations.

All these intervention measures can be grouped into more general categories, distinguishing the different strategies for 2000-2006 for EU policy. The menu approach, as stated earlier, is based on the choice between 24 different types of interventions in the EU rural development programmes. These interventions can be grouped in six broad categories of policy objectives:

Table 1. Intervention measures

Structural modernisation	This category includes: investments in agricultural holdings of EC Regulations (measure a), setting up of young farmers (meas. b), training (meas. c), early retirement (meas. d), improving processing and marketing of agricultural products (meas. g), re-parcelling (meas. k).
Support of environmental practices	This category includes: agri-environment (meas. f); re-forestation of agricultural land (meas. h); other forestry measures (meas. i); land improvement (meas. j); protection of environment in connection with agriculture, forestry and landscape conservation (meas. t); restoring agricultural production potential damaged by natural disasters and introducing appropriate prevention instruments (meas. u).
Development of infrastructures and services	This category includes: implementation of farm management services (meas. l); agricultural water resources management (meas. q); basic services for the economy and rural population (meas. n); development and improvement of infrastructure connected with the development of agriculture (meas. r).
Economic diversification	This category includes: marketing quality agricultural products (meas. m); renovation and improvement of villages and protection and conservation of the rural heritage (meas. o); diversification of agricultural activities and activities close to agriculture to provide multiple activities or alternative incomes (meas. p); to encourage tourism and crafts activities (meas. s).
Income support in less developed areas	This category is limited to compensatory allowances for less favoured areas and areas with environmental restrictions (measure e).

Figure 1. Distribution of rural development resources

(% of total resources by type of intervention in each EU country)

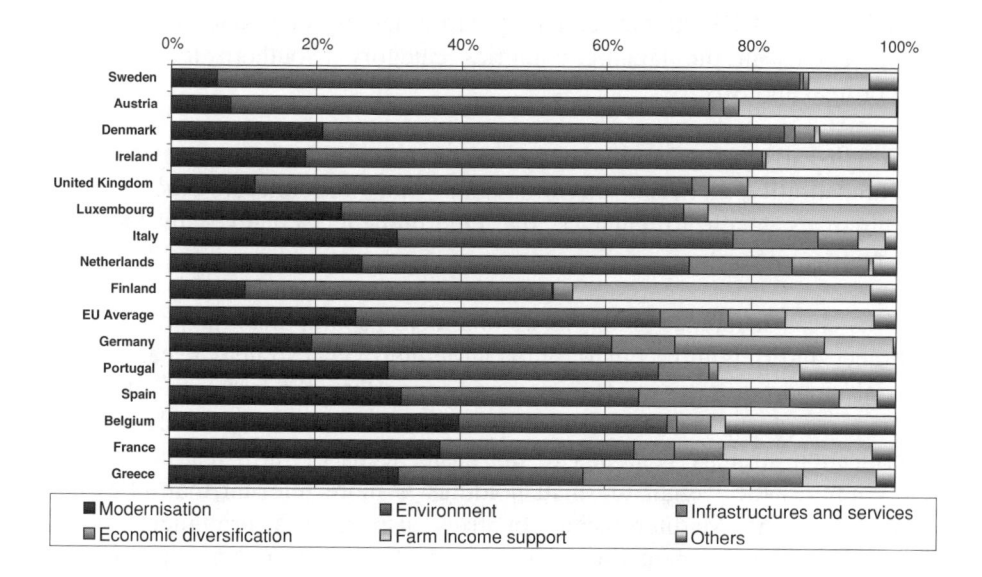

[Bar chart showing distribution across countries: Sweden, Austria, Denmark, Ireland, United Kingdom, Luxembourg, Italy, Netherlands, Finland, EU Average, Germany, Portugal, Spain, Belgium, France, Greece. Categories: Modernisation, Environment, Infrastructures and services, Economic diversification, Farm Income support, Others.]

Figure 1 shows how EU resources for 2000-2006 are being distributed among the different intervention measures. Global support of environmental practices can be seen to assume the largest portion of these interventions. When added to the structural modernisation incentives, they account for more than 66% of resources of RDP programmes. Rural development is mainly supported in the classical sense of modernisation and compensation for the higher costs associated with environmental practices. Economic diversification, instead, plays a more marginal role in the national and regional programmes.

What about the differences among countries and regions? Do objectives and strategies differ by country or by region? Which common profiles can be recognised by comparing the composition of public expenditures?

The main components of rural development strategies differ by both country and region. An analysis for RDPs from 2000 to 2006 in EU countries highlights different strategy models. Similar analyses have been developed by other researchers, with particular emphasis on the composition of the programmed expenditures (CNASEA, 2003; Dwyer et al 2002). Environmental practices always absorb a great amount of resources. Nevertheless, there are countries and groups of regions where modernisation is still a significant objective. Two groups of countries seem to emerge:

Mediterranean countries where modernisation has an important role in influencing RDP strategies. This group is largely dominated by countries or regions in the lagging countries category (Southern Italy, Greece, Portugal and Spain);

North-European countries where protection of the environment, compatibility between environmental and agricultural practices and initiatives taken to enhance the environmental context are the most important priorities.

This clear difference is not linked to a mere geographical factor. Countries like France and Belgium seem to follow a Mediterranean strategy because of the financial importance given to measures supporting the entrance of young farmers into farm management. Apart from France and Belgium, the modernisation strategy responds to the basic needs of farm restructuring. In these countries the weight of small holdings is more relevant than elsewhere (figure 3). Some Mediterranean countries also give a prominent role to infrastructure development due to the substantial support that irrigation and other collective infrastructures require in countries like Spain and Greece. Incentives for economic diversification confirm their marginal role almost everywhere, except in Eastern Germany. Conversely North-European countries have put considerable emphasis on the importance of the environment within their programmes, without taking into account the structural agriculture problems. Their strategy is essentially based on compensating a farmer's higher unitary costs with direct income supports if they adopt eco-compatible practices and/or they operate in special areas and continue to farm for a reasonable period of time[1].

---

[1] This second objective is supported by a specific compensatory allowance given to farmers in more disadvantaged areas or in environmentally sensitive areas (*i.e.* protected areas or under Nature 2000 directives).

Figure 2. Rural structural vs. environmental modernisation

In terms of development strategies

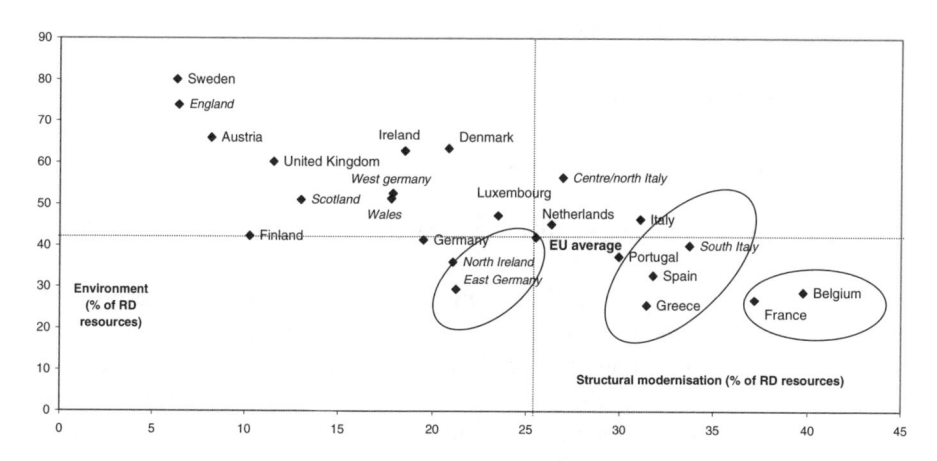

Figure 3. Modernisation measures in relation to holdings' structure

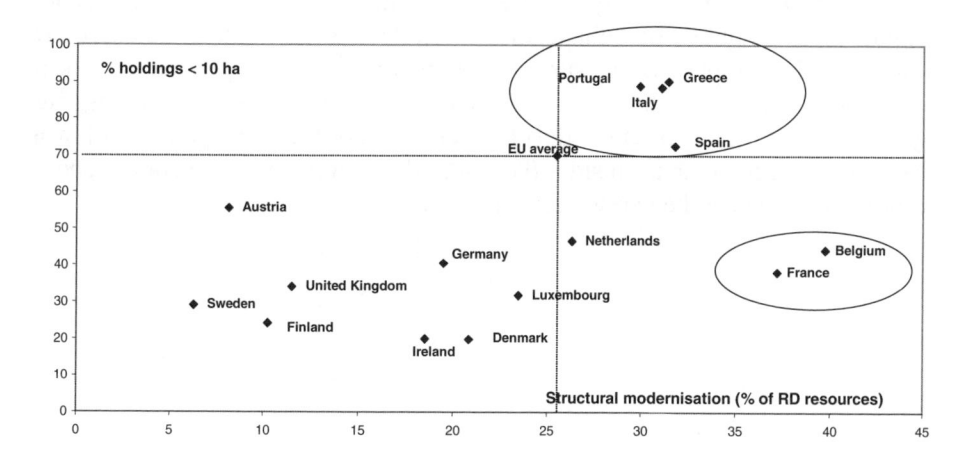

Another important issue within this analysis is the type of financial incentives used in rural development programmes. There is a strong and interesting debate on the role of different tools to promote local development. Recent economic literature on regional development in Italy (Barca, 1998; Viesti and Prota, 2004) outlines the growing importance and effectiveness of tools other than traditional firm-based incentives, which are more focused on the economic context at the local level. For this reason measures for rural development programmes have been classified into four broad categories[2]:

- Incentives for investments;

- Direct income support;

- Incentives for good practices;

- Incentives to enhance collective capital.

The first three categories address single farm units. The last focuses on the context surrounding the farm unit and concerns efforts aimed at enhancing conditions external to economic and social contexts. The distribution of financial resources among these categories of incentives is largely biased towards the first group of incentives. Those directed toward collective capital make up an average of only 23% of global EU resources (figure 4). The differences between countries here are similar to those that emerged earlier concerning rural development programmes. The Mediterranean countries[3], together with Eastern Germany and the Netherlands, follow a different strategy that puts more emphasis on enhancement of collective capital than do other EU countries. This approach to rural development, and in general to local development, seems to be more effective for solving problems in lagging regions. It works here because development factors tend to operate within a local context rather than inside the individual unit of production. These incentives can reduce the gap within external economies.

---

[2] This classification is different from the previous one because it focuses on the type of incentive used rather than on the objective of the support given by EU policy. In this sense it can be used as a complementary classification in this analysis.

[3] Apart from Portugal which does not follow this strategy.

Figure 4. Distribution of R&D resources

(among types of incentives in each EU country)

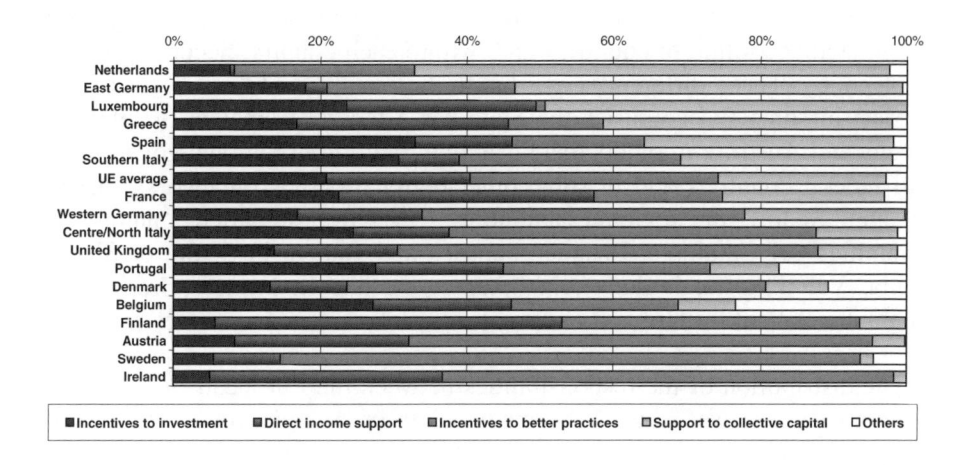

■ Incentives to investment ■ Direct income support ■ Incentives to better practices ◨ Support to collective capital ☐ Others

The role of institutions: decentralisation, partnerships and delivery systems

Relationships between the central level and the regional/local level have been increasingly changing in European countries (Bobbio, 2002; Caciagli, 2003). During the last decades there has been a process of institutional reform involving the state in most of European countries. One of the main common features of this process in Europe is that in the last decades regional institutions are gaining strength, particularly in traditionally centrally-oriented countries

Another common element is the process of reinforcing regional and local institutions which has been driven by various factors; one of the most important of which is the growing role of European regional policy. Since the Unique Act (1986), the EU has been strengthening and consolidating regional policies in order to reduce economic and social disparities among countries and regions. The main beneficiaries of such cohesion policy (financed by the so-called Structural Funds) are the regional and local governments. They have been forced to compete for funds to finance public investments for social and economic growth. Such competition is based on the preparation of good programmes and projects. Over time regional policies have stimulated growing competencies at regional and local levels in programming and government capacity, as well as further need for competencies and power at these levels;

While decentralisation is common, the related competencies in social and economic policy are very different across Europe. This process is still greatly differentiated according to countries and, within each country, according to the type of policy. These differences are due to the institutional framework of EU countries: in some EU countries the State has a federal framework (Belgium, Germany and Austria); in others there is a long tradition of regional government (in all federal countries and in some other regional-based frameworks like in Italy and Spain) or regional autonomy (*i.e.* the so-called "autonomy communities" of Catalonia, Basque countries and Galicia in Spain, or Sicily, Sardinia, Val d'Aosta, in Italy); in other cases, like in France, Greece and Portugal, the date of birth of some form of regional government is very recent.

The distribution of the responsibilities between the European Commission and member states was one of the main points of Agenda 2000. The model proposed by Agenda 2000 makes the Commission responsible for the co-ordination, control and general evaluation of the rural development policies co-financed by EU funds. Member states and Regions are responsible for defining programmes and implementing rural development measures. Even following the changes of Agenda 2000, the Commission still retains strong competencies and decision-making powers, maintaining a strong influence on the quality and overall strategy of the rural development policies.

The degree of decentralisation of rural development policies is strongly differentiated according to country. Rural development policies are largely centralised in many European countries. Despite the strong favour given to regional authorities by Agenda 2000, rural development still remains largely under national and central control. This is evident when looking at the competencies in rural development programmes in EU-15 (table 2) or at traditionally centralised countries like France, Ireland and all Scandinavian countries. It seems surprising however, in countries like Austria and the Netherlands where regional agricultural authorities have well-established competencies. The only countries with fully decentralised competencies are Germany and Italy, where they only have regional programmes. Some of the centrally-run countries are quite small, so there is a certain justification for the central planning. For others a national plan is justified by the rationality of management at the central level, the biggest being France along with Austria and Sweden with their long traditions of decentralisation. The degree of decentralisation is higher for rural development supported under the EAGGF-Guidance section, under Structural Funds within the regional policy.

Table 2. **National vs. regional competences in rural development**

(Concerning management of programmes in European countries)

Country	Competences in rural development system
LUXEMBOURG	Exclusively national
DENMARK	
SWEDEN	
FRANCE	Prevailing national
IRELAND	
AUSTRIA	
The NETHERLANDS	
FINLAND	Mixed with national dominance
PORTUGAL	
GREECE	
SPAIN	Mixed with regional dominance
BELGIUM	
UNITED KINGDOM	
GERMANY	Regional
ITALY	

Figure 5. National vs. regional distribution of RDP resources

(% in each EU country)

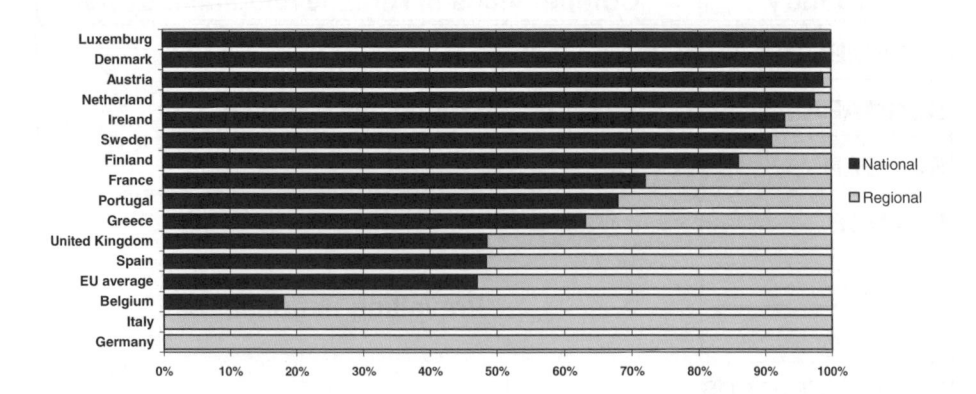

[Bar chart showing National vs Regional distribution for countries: Luxemburg, Denmark, Austria, Netherland, Ireland, Sweden, Finland, France, Portugal, Greece, United Kingdom, Spain, EU average, Belgium, Italy, Germany]

The same conclusion can be drawn when we look at resource distribution among States and Regions within the EU-15 (figure 5). An EU average shows that for total rural development resources, half

centrally managed and the other half is regionally managed. More than 70% of resources are centrally managed in France, Ireland, Scandinavian countries, Austria, the Netherlands, and Luxembourg. Spain and the United Kingdom are very close to this average[4]. Germany and Italy are confirmed as the most decentralised countries in Europe (with 100% of the resources delivered by regions).

In order to understand the efficiency and the effectiveness of the institutional system in the field of rural development interventions, more attention should be given to the delivery system used. From the analysis of the

---

[4] The case of United Kingdom seems very particular when compared with the other countries in this respect. Here we have four big "regions": Northern Ireland, Scotland, Wales and England. The first three can be considered comparable with the other European regions, both in terms of territorial size and in terms of resources managed. However, the case of England is strongly different, because it is more similar to the other EU States, whatever comparison might be considered.

Italian implementation of rural development programmes, we can see that three fundamental models are emerging. These models can also be found in other European countries[5].

The three models can be defined as follows:

1. Dispersion model;

2. Unbalanced model;

3. Balanced model.

The first model is represented in Figure 6. The main characteristics of this model are the presence of an abundance of measures in each rural development programme and the lack of integration and links among measures (each measure is managed independently from the other and it follows its own rules and procedures). This shapes the main outcome of the model: each single investment/public intervention is scattered over the regional territory. The word "dispersion" is used here to identify policies which are distributed over a large territory. This means a low global impact of rural development measures on regional areas.

Figure 6. The dispersion model

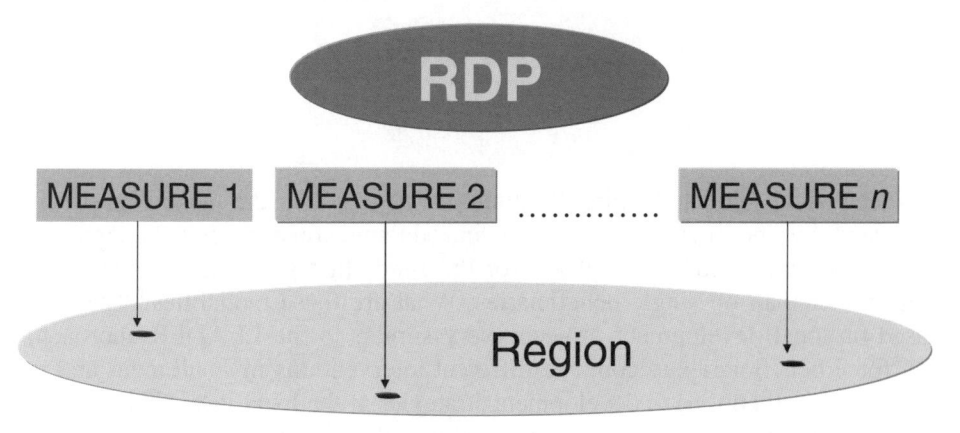

---

[5] I presented these models in a seminar held in Wilton Park Conference on "Investing in the Future of Rural Areas in Europe" (16-19 February 2004) and there colleagues from different European countries confirmed some of conclusions drawn from this presentation.

The second model is represented in Figure 7. This model is to some extent similar to the first one as it results in the lack of integration and links among measures. But there is a crucial difference: in regions where there are strong disparities among rural areas, the intensity of demand and political pressures focused on public policies push resources toward the richest areas. This means that public investments and interventions are focused on these areas, rather than on the most marginal ones. As a result the impact on the marginal areas is very low. This contributes to reinforcing territorial disparities within the region and is why it is referred to as "unbalanced".

Figure 7. The unbalanced model

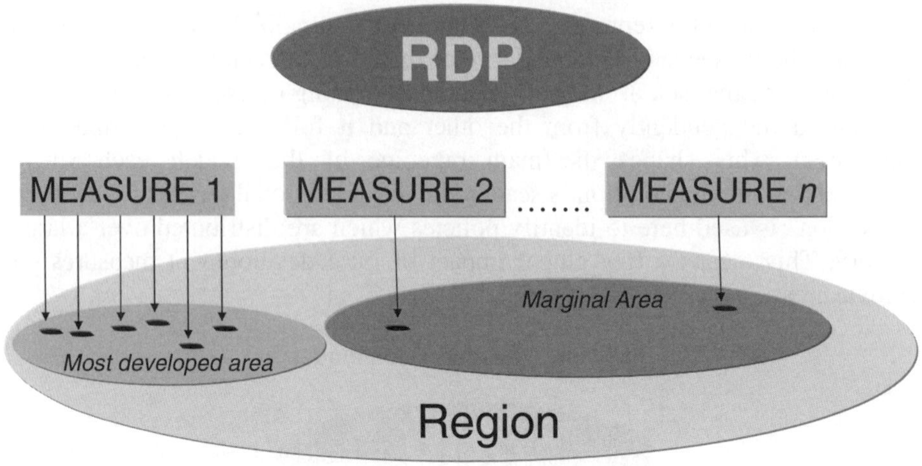

The final model, Figure 8, attempts to resolve the negative effects generated by the previous model by introducing some form of integration among measures and of modalities for the funds that government focuses on areas rather than on single beneficiaries. What are these modalities? They are based on local development projects (very similar to the LEADER approach) that force beneficiaries to combine different interventions in small areas and to link these interventions to development strategies at the local level. This implies higher impacts on single areas and positive effects on territorial disparities within the region. But there are several important conditions to be fulfilled in order to apply this model, which can be summarised as follows:

- Stronger focus on territorial/thematic priorities than on measures;

- Gradual reduction of sectoral and individual incentives and more focus on the local context;

- Decentralisation, but with strong support from the central level (*i.e.* technical assistance for local partnerships, to monitor and evaluate, etc.);

- Opportunity to integrate different funds (at the programming level) and to combine different resources and tools (at the project level);

- Financial flexibility, both at the programme and project level.

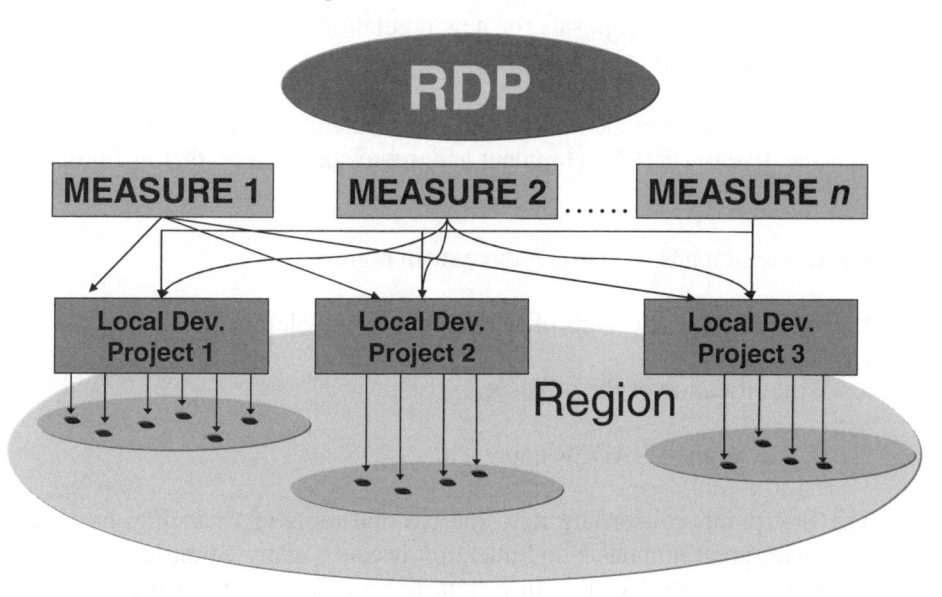

Figure 8. The balanced model

What are the prospects for future EU rural development policy reform (after 2006)?

In the previous pages we tried to highlight the main weaknesses and strengths that came out of the Agenda 2000 reform of the EU rural development policies for 2000 to 2006. These issues are now on the agenda for the mid-term review of CAP and, at the same time, on the agenda for the next programming period from 2007 to 2013. For this latter period a new, more substantial reform process has to be conceived. This reform process was introduced during the

European Conference held in Salzburg in December 2003 and has since continued on several different occasions:

- Mid Term Review of CAP presentation and approval (end of 2003 to the beginning of 2004);

- Proposals from the European Commission on the new financial perspectives for the enlarged Europe 2007-2013 (February 2004);

- Third report on social and economic cohesion (February 2004);

- European Forum on cohesion (May 2004);

- Finally during proposals for new regulations for Structural Funds and Rural Development (July 2004).

These materials provide enough information for ample discussion of the future perspective of rural development and, more specifically, that of European policy.

The discussion has focused on three main points:

1. New sources and tools of financing rural development;

2. Simplification of the policies;

3. Future of the LEADER approach.

The first point, concerning new sources and tools of financing, has been discussed with great emphasis and attention because many countries asked for substantial steps forward in this direction. Main solutions that were proposed can be summarised as follows:

- Level of financial support for rural development will remain as it is now (in real terms);

- Financial support will be maintained for all rural areas in Europe, but with the intensity of public aids to be differentiated according to the general level of social and economic development;

- Only one financial tool will be introduced for all rural development programmes in Europe, avoiding the inefficient and complicated distinction between different sources existing at the present moment between lagging regions and other regions.

There is an important aspect that should be stressed within the new reform project: the new Rural Development Fund will no longer be part of the Structural Funds. This will have subsequent implications in terms of relationships and co-ordination with the regional policies.

The second point, addressing the simplification of policies, has been emphasized especially by France and the new Member States. There are three issue types addressing this point:

- Each country or region only needs one rural development plan instead of having different programming documents financed by the EU funds;

- Introduction of rules that derive their efficiency criteria from the previous Rural Development and Structural Funds mechanisms (the new rules will be a sort of mixture of the rules governing rural Funds and Structural Funds);

- More flexibility in the programming and management processes;

- Strengthen the monitoring, evaluation and control tools in order to improve the effectiveness of public aid.

Finally, the LEADER approach has become the mainstream approach for new rural development programmes[6] (evident in other EU Initiatives such as EQUAL and URBAN).

What are main implications of these proposals on future rural development policies? Implications are clearly positive in terms of simplification. However final evaluation of the new reform design should also take into consideration the broader expected and unexpected outcomes.

First the idea of separating rural development from the cohesion policies seems to be particularly negative. Rural development in the future of EU policy will be independent from other cohesion policies financed by

---

[6] At the present moment LEADER has its own programme and small financial endowments in order to guarantee that the approach is applied in all European countries.

Structural Funds, with their own programmes and rules and thus isolated from the other policies. Furthermore, this separation will make rural development policies more divided into sectors and more modernisation-focused than they are now. This will further reduce the diversification component of the programmes (that, as previously noted, received little attention in current programmes).

Secondly, from this reform project it emerges that the integration principle has no future. It seems that the integration of tools and funds has been deemed a source of inefficiency for EU policies. This conclusion seems very inappropriate and strange. Many innovative projects in the field of rural development and regional development were set up to take advantage of the possibility of integrating funds and sectors. This opportunity has resulted in a number of successful integrated regional programmes that combine funds and interventions in different sectors. This has proven to work and thus should be embraced, not discarded for its seeming complexity.

Finally, the idea of mainstreaming LEADER seems very interesting as it has proven to be functional as a major mechanism for the diffusion of this new approach to rural development. In addition to this proof, it is crucial to devote a special portion of resources to this programme in order to encourage national or regional administrations to allocate high financial importance to LEADER within their new rural programmes.

BIBLIOGRAPHY

1. Beccattini Giacomo (2000), Dal distretto industriale allo sviluppo locale, Bollati Boringhieri, Torino.

2. Bagnasco Arnaldo (1977), Tre Italie. La problematica territoriale dello sviluppo italiano, Il Mulino, Bologna.

3. Bagnasco Arnaldo (2003), Società fuori squadra. Come cambia l'organizzazione sociale, Il Mulino, Bologna.

4. Caciagli Mario, Regioni d'Europa. Devoluzioni, regionalismi, integrazione europea, Il Mulino, Bologna, 2003.

5. CNASEA (2003), L'application du reglement de developpement rural en Europe, Les cahiers du Cnasea, n. 3, Paris.

6. Dwyer J., Baldock D., Beaufoy G., Bennett H., Lowe P., Ward N., (2002), Europe's Rural future. The nature of rural development II: Rural Development in an Enlarging European Union, Comparative Report.

7. Garofoli Gioacchino (1991), Modelli locali di sviluppo, Milano, F.Angeli.

8. Garofoli Gioacchino (2003), (a cura di), Impresa e territorio, Il Mulino, Bologna.

9. Iacoponi Luciano (1990), Distretto industriale marshalliano e forme dell' organizzazione delle imprese in agricoltura, Rivista di economia agraria, n.4.

10. Mantino Francesco (1995) (a cura di), Impresa agraria e dintorni. Contributi allo studio dell'impresa e delle sue trasformazioni nel territorio, Studi e ricerche INEA, Roma.

11. Ministero del Tesoro, Bilancio e Programmazione Economica (1998), La nuova programmazione e il Mezzogiorno, Donzelli, Roma.

12. Viesti Gianfranco e Prota Francesco (2004), Le politiche regionali dell'Unione Europea, Il Mulino, Bologna.

PART III: THE FUTURE OF RURAL POLICY

Five Themes in the Future of Rural Policy
by Mark Drabenstott

Vice-President and Director
Center for the Study of Rural America
Federal Reserve Bank of Kansas City
United States

The dialogue at the conference was certainly stimulating and rich. While there is still much work to do in forging a new vision for rural policy, this conference provided a sturdy springboard to the future. Five themes particularly resonated with me. I would like to briefly touch on each, and also try to show some links among them, since putting together all the pieces into a compelling vision is the biggest challenge we face as we move forward to a new generation of rural policy.

The first theme is globalization and the new rural geography. There is little doubt that globalization is the driving force behind the quest for new rural policies. The dramatic impacts of globalizing markets are coming home in regions. That this topic launched the dialogue here is no surprise. What may be more interesting is the fact that more and more rural regions in the United States already understand the imperative of globalizing markets, and I suspect the same is true elsewhere around the globe. A ground swell of new rural regions is forming throughout rural America. Last year, about twenty multi-county regions contacted our Center seeking help on new economic development efforts. Representing north, south, east, and west, the regions are very diverse in their economics and demographics. But they all have one thing in common—they understand that they must build new economic engines because globalization is taking away the old ones.

A vanguard of leaders in rural regions has seized this new rural imperative before most rural policy makers. While the conference has highlighted several noteworthy innovations in rural policy, existing rural policies still have a powerful inertia behind them. Sooner or later, globalization will change that, too. Existing rural policies assume the ubiquity of rural industries like agriculture or manufacturing. New rural policies must embrace a much more diverse rural economy. There is no longer one economic tide to lift all boats. The new rural economy will be much more complex—a new competitive advantage for every region. For regions and for policy makers, the magic will come in finding the right competitive advantage—and the right policy to support it. This demands far more flexibility, and much more responsibility at the regional level than the policies to which we are accustomed.

The second theme is the new rural economy. Throughout the conference, we have heard encouraging tales of rural regions that are breaking away from old economic engines and building new ones. The U.S. countryside too is dotted with signs of promise. Yet here, as in other countries, I suspect those signs are too sporadic to represent a wave sweeping all or even most regions to new prosperity. All too frequently, commodity industries are deeply entrenched, and many regions continue to believe that cheap land and labour are still their chief economic assets. In most OECD countries, that era is past.

Building a new rural economy is framed by daunting challenge and tantalizing opportunity. But the situation is not balanced. The challenges are plain while the opportunities are often veiled. We need to be clear in how we view the "new" rural economy. It is "new" because it is driven by "new" markets. Those markets may be products and services exported from the region to buyers elsewhere. Or it may be using the amenities of the region to bring consumers to the region.

Either way, rural regions must produce what will sell, not sell what they produce. Welch's is a terrific story of this principle at work. Tapping these new markets will take entrepreneurs and fresh policy approaches. An essential aspect of the new policies will be robust analytics that help regions assess markets with the greatest promise for their distinct set of economic assets. Those analytics are in extremely short supply.

Entrepreneurs will play a central role in building the new rural economy. If the United States is indicative, over the past half century, rural regions have been too focused on recruiting businesses while overlooking the need to tend to home-grown companies. More and more rural regions are now beginning to understand that entrepreneurs not only build the new rural economy, they also help regions discover their true niche in global markets. But while entrepreneurs are moving centre stage in the rural economy, they remain on the fringes of rural policy. That must change if new policies are to be effective.

The third theme is innovations in governance. If regions have become the new unit of rural policy, governance has become the new frontier. Most rural regions have jurisdictional lines drawn for a very different economy. In the U.S., many county lines were drawn with horse and wagon in mind—the distance a farmer could drive to the county seat and return before sundown. Here again, past rigidities must give way to new flexibilities. Twenty-first century opportunities will not respect the surveyors of earlier generations. Yet we are constantly reminded of how limiting those lines can be in forging the partnerships needed for successful development strategies.

Who plays the role of catalyst in innovating regional governance? That is a critical question going forward. Here in the United States, we are currently focusing on three candidates for change: government, higher education, and the private sector, including businesses and non-profit organizations. One of these three groups must be the governance "innovator" in the region. If no one does, the region is likely to stagnate. Thus far, our research suggests that higher education and philanthropic groups are most often the catalyst. It will be important for policy makers to consider the role for government as a regional catalyst—as well as their role in providing new incentives for public and private actors to partner at a regional level. Such incentives are a powerful tool, and many of the discussions at this conference illustrate how far we still have to go in tapping that power.

The fourth theme is transition. There was strong agreement that new rural policies are needed. We are much less clear on how to get there, especially given the policies that are now in place. Two points are worth stressing as we look to the future.

First, new policies need new constituencies. By and large, the need for new rural policies is outrunning the formation of new rural stakeholder groups. While that suggests the stakeholders will ultimately galvanize, many rural regions will suffer economically in the interim. Will rural people give new voice to the need for rural policy? And will this case compel the majority? These critical questions are, by and large, still unanswered.

In the end, though, new policies also need new champions. In virtually every example of policy innovation that we have considered over the past two days, a visionary public leader invested political capital to innovate rural policy. Such champions are scarce, but there are more than first meets the eye. Our conversations with public policy groups throughout the nation suggest that more and more public entrepreneurs are emerging. These entrepreneurs understand the need for change. They have the will to change. What they often do not have is the analysis to rebut the status quo.

To give but one example, the most prevalent development strategy in rural America today is business recruitment. Billions of dollars are spent every year by state and local governments to lure companies to the countryside. Globalization puts more and more of those recruitment incentives at risk. Unfortunately, my fellow economists have not been as thorough as they could have been in evaluating the true costs of this recruitment race, nor in pointing out the benefits of growing more local entrepreneurs. In short, this is a time for visionary public leaders with state-of-the-art information.

The final theme is synergy. Throughout the conference, we have seen examples of new rural policies that harness the power of other existing policies, and create a whole that is bigger than the sum of its parts. In every rural region of the world, transportation, health, and education policies are already at work. What is needed is a coherent link between existing policies, with the overall aim to help rural regions build new competitive advantages. It is this overarching aim that is the biggest missing piece of the puzzle, and thus the one with the greatest value. Our challenge is to knit together existing policies, integrate some missing pieces, all the while recognizing that the picture that emerges will be different in every region. This task seems daunting, but the past two days have provided some real glimpses into the fact that it can be done.

Another aspect of synergy should not be lost. New rural policies have several benefits going for them in light of other policy conundrums facing developed nations. The outcome of last fall's WTO talks in Cancun leave little doubt that agricultural policies are thorny obstacles to progress toward freer trade. If better ways can be found to boost the wellbeing of farmers and rural residents, we can imagine a future with fewer trade disputes and stronger rural economies.

Lastly, new rural policies may well prove to have more bang for the buck than existing policies. Although the conference was certainly not conclusive on this point, a number of presenters stressed the investment aspect of the new policies as opposed to the subsidy aspect of the old. This suggests there could be sizable fiscal dividends awaiting the adoption of new policies. In Washington as in other capitals, surely that is welcome news.

Where is Rural Policy Headed?
by Sergio Soto Priante

General Co-ordinator of Micro-Regions
Ministry of Social Development
Mexico

One of the key issues that policy makers need to address when it comes to increasing competitiveness in rural areas is the necessity to involve all social actors in the process. NGOs, private foundations, business organizations and universities can provide input that can facilitate the development processes. Public funds devoted to support valuable projects from such organizations can enhance the reach of public policies.

Local based strategies should utilize a bottom-up approach that transfers the responsibility of development from the central and regional government to the local authorities and the communities. We consider such an approach a critical element that needs to be emphasized through creative public policies. This approach requires a change of culture and consequently a role change for local partners, moving them from mere spectators to main actors. The intervention of an external development agent can promote synergies that are otherwise difficult to achieve.

A continuous evaluation process to assess the impact of rural policies will be critical to ensuring proper allocation of resources and provide legislators with proof to justify their confidence in territorial based rural development strategies and programmes. Fostering new, fresh, local leadership facilitates the promotion of entrepreneurship, the development of strong social capital and the commitment of communities to their own future. Also, the introduction of innovative technologies in rural areas has been highlighted as a shortcut in rural development that might need a more in-depth discussion.

Because of the diversity among regions, flexibility has to be a strong characteristic of rural policy. It is the task of local actors to adopt and adapt policies so that they fit in every region's reality. Emphasis should be put on the general principles that enable local or regional characteristics to flourish.

Another major task that successful rural policies require is improvement in local authorities' skills in strategic planning and their ability to identify opportunities in inter-municipal projects and regional strategies.

When Franco Mantino dealt with the risk in the future of regional policies in the EU, he noted among others the "prevalence of sectoral objectives". Such risk may exist also in other OECD countries out of the EU area, and might require a major effort, even in the design or redesign of some governmental institutions, in order to make viable the coexistence of territorial and sectorial objectives.

The concept of social economy or social responsible economy was mentioned several times during this conference, and though it is not a new topic, it merits further discussion. Another subject that attracted my attention is the role that cooperatives have to play as a vehicle of rural development.

Finally I would like to stress the importance of shared information among policy makers, and invite you all to the international conference that the Mexican Ministry of Social Development and the OECD will be hosting in Oaxaca, Mexico in 2005, where we expect to evaluate our progress and continue this discussion on new approaches to rural policy.

Challenges for the Future of Rural Policy
by Richard Wakeford

Chief Executive
The Countryside Agency
United Kingdom

Over the past few years we have seen an increasing convergence of view. Agriculture must be regarded as part of the overall rural policy and a more integrated approach to rural territorial development is required.

In the Common Agricultural Policy (CAP) reform, soon to be implemented, and in the US Farm Bill, there is a welcome shift away from subsidies for growing commodities and towards paying for public benefits. Those public benefits may, but only may, help to strengthen the distinctive qualities of rural areas to help them develop stronger businesses in the future. These businesses range from those serving markets with the niche products they can provide such as the total experience of food, hotel stays, landscape enjoyment and use of trails publicly maintained, or more distant markets for special products such as Spanish tiles.

So, we have a clear view of where we are aiming for now, how will we get there? The choice will be determined by each nation according to their cultures and constitutions, political and civil service, NGOs and other agents, businesses and so on.

First we have to set strategy in the context of the outside drivers that will affect our rural pitch and acknowledge that there will be changes. We need to concentrate on getting the details right, particularly at the stage of identifying which distinctive assets to promote. One detail is to ensure that you get your policies designed to suit the type of countryside. For example, England does not have much remote rural, yet it does have a sizable population concerned with rural policy, conserving and exploiting the landscape asset, providing access to services, especially for those without cars, and facilitating access to affordable rural housing. The same characteristics can be seen in rural New Jersey and in most of Maryland. This may be due to a social remoteness people feel in densely populated areas causing an attachment and increased attention over a diminishing, pressured rural environment. However in Sweden, and Kansas in the US, the population distribution is quite different. In these areas policies need to address physical remoteness and sparseness of population. Another geographical classification is about the quality of space. National Parks and Areas of Outstanding Natural Beauty (AONB) require a different approach as the higher quality environment increases the attraction to live there, or run businesses. So, not all rural is the same but there are lessons to be learned regions with similar countryside types.

My next cautionary note is migration. Population growth and world instability are causing people to move and, though this is not just a rural phenomenon, rural areas are affected by this global pressure. The migration picture for England shows that people are willing to move to the countryside for the products available. However the population migrating to the countryside is different from the existing population, often wealthier, white, middle class and middle-aged. This presents rural areas with a challenge to find a solution that meets the needs of these two populations. A concentrated affluent community presents a market opportunity for rural areas to offer new commercial and service provisions. At the same time it is equally important to note that these differences can put the current residents at a disadvantage. As the new population is more mobile and prepared to travel for goods and services, there is a diminished market for rural service provision. Even with rural proofing, it is hard to protect the original country people. We must also consider that some countryside in Europe and in the US is losing population. This presents a need for different policy, one where younger people are encouraged to stay by increased economic or educational opportunity.

The movement of goods also has a sizable impact on rural communities. Globalisation and improving transportation open the world to new sources of food. As long as fuel remains cheap old rural areas will need to find innovative ways are to respond to the new world order. In addition, this increased movement has a dangerous side-effect, global warming. We must factor in the impacts of increased temperature around the world and develop alternate responses, such as increased use of renewable energy as we strategize for rural areas.

Another phenomenon is the adverse health effects caused by inactivity. This presents a potential opportunity for the countryside towns adjacent to densely populated regions to offer infrastructure for people's physical and mental health. The Countryside Agency has led the way in this through its "Walking the Way to Health" initiative involving the British Heart Foundation and step-o-meters through which we are all urged to take 10,000 steps a day.

At the Countryside Agency we have also implemented the "Eat the View" program. We believe that as the world gets richer, consumers will want to spend more on quality food, not quantity. The growing organic sector is demonstrative of this hypothesis. Not everyone wants ever bigger carrots if they taste less good, not all carrots are equal. Though organic production is a more labour intensive process we can encourage farmers to add more value through quality, even if it means fewer bushels per acre. Farms near urban areas may have a particular opportunity here to sell their overall package of food, landscape and community engagement. Economists will need to find a way of measuring this production in ways other than bushels per acre to encourage this activity. The more people "Eat the View", the more they can engage in delivering the quality of countryside that is clearly in demand.

The importance of agriculture and farm policy can be seen as part of an overall rural policy, and not separate initiatives. Nowhere was that more apparent than in our experience of Foot and Mouth Disease. This had wider impacts on the economy – not just agriculture. The risk of disease is ever higher as trade increases, especially informal trade. As a result the whole rural economy needs to be ready should the problem arise again.

Finally, the countryside offers an opportunity for organic waste disposal. In a number of countries there is an over-dependence on landfill, whereas farmers could well diversify further into helping urban areas deal with this waste.

All of this leads me to the following conclusions about the direction of rural policy. The direction of rural policy should be towards greater integration of sectoral approaches whether they are in food, tourism services, landscape or public benefits. Policy should focus on capitalizing upon local distinctiveness and niche urban markets, be it with food or non-food products, which the rural area can supply. Commodity subsidies should be replaced with payments for sustainable land management and could be supplemented with incentives for businesses that benefit from those landscapes and nature conservation. Local empowerment should be encouraged to drive innovation and local-level partnerships. Opportunities should be leveraged to attract migrants, particularly for new rural jobs, by marketing town clusters rather than factory parks. Rural rights should be protected through rural proofing. There should be a push toward more engagement between town and country, by purchasing farm products, paying for public benefits, using common spaces for exercise and relaxation, educating tomorrow's consumers, securing rural services, *etc*. Most importantly we need not lose sight of the need to plan to deal with threats such as animal disease that may have much wider impacts on the rural order.

ANNEX A:
CONFERENCE PROGRAM

THE NEED FOR NEW RURAL POLICIES

INTRODUCTORY REMARKS AND MODERATOR

Thomas M. Hoenig - President and Chief Executive Officer, Federal Reserve
Bank of Kansas City, United States

WELCOMING REMARKS

Constance A. Morella - U.S. Ambassador to the Organisation for Economic Cooperation and Development (OECD), Paris

THINKING REGIONALLY IN A GLOBALIZING ECONOMY

Alan Greenspan - Chairman, Board of Governors of the Federal Reserve System, United States

THE NEW ECONOMIC IMPERATIVE IN RURAL REGIONS

Donald J. Johnston - Secretary-General, OECD, Paris

DISCUSSION PANEL

Antonio Sánchez de Rivera - Vice Minister, Ministry of Social Development, Mexico
Oryssia J. Lennie - Deputy Minister, Western Economic Diversification, Canada
Gianfranco Miccicché - Deputy Minister, Ministry of the Economy, Italy

THE VISION FOR NEW RURAL POLICIES

INTRODUCTORY REMARKS AND MODERATOR

David A. Sampson - Assistant Secretary for Economic Development, Department of Commerce, United States

A NEW FRAMEWORK FOR RURAL POLICY

Mario Pezzini - Head, Division of Territorial Reviews and Governance, OECD, Paris

DISCUSSION PANEL

Wendi Key - Assistant Secretary, Regional Programmes Operations, Department of Transport and Regional Services, Australia
Kees de Ruiter - Director, Department of Rural Policy, Ministry of Agriculture, Nature, and Food Quality, Netherlands
Nicolas Jacquet - President, Territorial Planning and Regional Action, France

THE RURAL POLICY LABORATORY AROUND THE GLOBE: BUILDING A NEW RURAL ECONOMY

INTRODUCTORY REMARKS AND MODERATOR

Margaret Clark - Director, The Countryside Agency, United Kingdom

AMENITY-BASED DEVELOPMENT

Norio Sato - Director of Rural Policy, Rural Development Bureau, Ministry of Agriculture, Forestry, and Fisheries, Japan

RURAL ENTREPRENEURSHIP

C. Robert Militello - Director, National Grape Association, Inc., and WelchFoods, Inc., United States

DEVELOPING NEW RURAL INDUSTRIES

Francesco Mantino - Head, Structural Policies and Rural Development, National Institute for Agriculture Economics, Italy

THE RURAL POLICY LABORATORY AROUND THE GLOBE: RETHINKING GOVERNANCE

INTRODUCTORY REMARKS AND MODERATOR

Charles W. Fluharty - Director, Rural Policy Research Institute, United States

RURAL PROOFING

John Mills - Director of Rural Policy, Department for the Environment, Food, and Rural Affairs, United Kingdom

NEW REGIONAL PARTNERSHIPS

Gilbert Gonzalez, Jr. - Acting Under Secretary for Rural Development, Department of Agriculture, United States

FEDERAL CO-ORDINATION

Wolf Huber - Director, Regional Policy and Spatial Planning, Federal Chancellery, Austria

WHERE IS RURAL POLICY HEADED?

INTRODUCTORY REMARKS AND MODERATOR

Odile Sallard - Director, Directorate of Public Governance and Territorial Development, OECD, Paris

CLOSING PANEL

Fabrizio Barca - Head, Department for Development Policies, Ministry of the Economy, Italy
Mark Drabenstott - Vice President and Director, Center for the Study of Rural America, Federal Reserve Bank of Kansas City, United States
Sergio Soto Priante - General Co-ordinator of Micro Regions, Ministry of Social Development, Mexico
Richard Wakeford - Chief Executive, The Countryside Agency, United Kingdom

OECD PUBLICATIONS, 2, rue André-Pascal, 75775 PARIS CEDEX 16
PRINTED IN FRANCE
(04 2005 05 1 P) ISBN 92-64-01012-2 – No. 54037 2005